ANNUAL UPDATE **2022**

US POLITICS

Sarra Jenkins
Emma Kilheeney McSherry

HODDER
EDUCATION
AN HACHETTE UK COMPANY

Every effort has been made to trace all copyright holders, but if any have been inadvertently overlooked, the Publishers will be pleased to make the necessary arrangements at the first opportunity.

Although every effort has been made to ensure that website addresses are correct at time of going to press, Hodder Education cannot be held responsible for the content of any website mentioned in this book. It is sometimes possible to find a relocated web page by typing in the address of the home page for a website in the URL window of your browser.

Hachette UK's policy is to use papers that are natural, renewable and recyclable products and made from wood grown in well-managed forests and other controlled sources. The logging and manufacturing processes are expected to conform to the environmental regulations of the country of origin.

Orders: please contact Hachette UK Distribution, Hely Hutchinson Centre, Milton Road, Didcot, Oxfordshire, OX11 7HH. Telephone: +44 (0)1235 827827. Email education@hachette.co.uk. Lines are open from 9 a.m. to 5 p.m., Monday to Friday. You can also order through our website: www.hoddereducation.co.uk

ISBN: 978 1 3983 6120 1

© Sarra Jenkins and Emma Kilheeney McSherry 2022

First published in 2022 by
Hodder Education,
An Hachette UK Company
Carmelite House
50 Victoria Embankment
London EC4Y 0DZ
www.hoddereducation.co.uk

Impression number   5 4 3 2 1
Year   2026 2025 2024 2023 2022

Cover photo © Piotr Pawinski - stock.adobe.com

Illustrations by Aptara, Inc.

Typeset in India by Aptara, Inc.

Printed in the UK

A catalogue record for this title is available from the British Library.

Contents

Chapter 1

The growing challenge of federalism

Context

- Federalism is a key principle of the US Constitution. While the word itself does not appear in the Constitution, it can be seen in action in a number of places, such as through the amendment process and the Tenth Amendment.
- Federalism means 'shared sovereignty'. In constitutional terms, this means that power in the USA is shared between states and the federal (or national) government, each of which have their own areas of responsibility.
- It was important to the Founding Fathers that federalism was included in the Constitution as their experience of a large central government was a negative one. The British had taxed the 13 American colonies without offering them representation in Parliament. They wanted to avoid repeating history in writing the Constitution.
- The 'elastic clause' in the Constitution has allowed Congress to expand the powers that are explicitly given to it. This, along with interpretations of the Constitution's 7,000 words by the Supreme Court, has allowed the growth of federal government over time, sometimes at the expense of the powers of states.
- In the twenty-first century, the issue of federalism has been a problem for both Republican and Democratic presidents. Under G. W. Bush, a new department was established (Homeland Security) which increased the size of federal government. Under Obama, the Patient Protection and Affordable Care Act (Obamacare) required all Americans to have healthcare insurance, whether they or their state wanted it. Trump fought with Congress for federal funding for his border wall. Each of these represented a blow to state power and sovereignty.
- The events of 2020–21 have brought to the fore a number of issues regarding federalism — abortion in Texas, the statehood of Washington DC and developments in marijuana policy under the Biden administration.
- With President Biden taking office at a time when US politics is highly divided (known as hyper-partisanship), some states have sought to assert their power against the new Democratic administration.

Exam success

AQA	3.2.1.1	The constitutional framework of government
	3.2.1.8	Civil rights
Edexcel	1	The US Constitution and federalism
	4	US Supreme Court and civil rights

It is crucial that students understand what the word 'federalism' means. It is a word that is new to many Politics students and too few are able to define it. It means 'shared sovereignty'. The Constitution is sovereign in US politics, and this document divides powers and roles between the states and the national government. For example, state governments have the right to determine whether they want to use the death penalty or not, and what form of it they wish to use, but the federal government (Congress, president and Supreme Court) controls foreign policy. The balance of this power changes over time, but is also dependent on the issue at hand — abortion, for example, has been a key issue in 2021.

A common misconception among students is a lack of understanding of the importance of states in the everyday life of citizens. Much of the specification focuses on federal-level politics and the three key branches of government. However, for most US citizens, their daily lives are likely to be more affected by the state they live in than by the federal government. It is impossible to know the differences between all 50 states, but good knowledge of one state can be invaluable in providing examples to use in an exam. After all, there is only one federal government while there are 50 state governments — and thousands of local governments under those!

The best students will understand that state governments often mirror the set-up of the federal government. At the top they have a governor and they often have a state congress, which usually has two houses, and a state supreme court. Well-informed students will know that the laws that state government passes can affect almost every aspect of a citizen's life, and the chances of the federal government overruling such laws are relatively limited.

For both Edexcel (12-mark essays) and AQA (25-mark essays), you should be able to compare federalism in the USA with devolution in the UK. This includes understanding the extent of the power of states in the USA and of devolved bodies in the UK and being able to analyse how secure the powers of these bodies are. For Edexcel, you could also face a 30-mark question on the topic of federalism alone, or as part of a wider question about the effectiveness of the US constitutional democracy. It is important to evaluate in such questions the ever-changing flow of power in federalism, demonstrating that the extent of state power can vary over time or over an issue.

Abortion in Texas

One of the key battlegrounds that provides insight into the nature of federalism in 2021 has been the issue of abortion in Texas, which has banned the use of abortions after 6 weeks of pregnancy. The appointment of three conservative Supreme Court justices by Donald Trump had already raised concerns over the security of abortion rights in the USA (see Chapter 5). This right is drawn from the case of *Roe* v *Wade* in 1973, in which the Supreme Court's interpretation constitutionally guaranteed a woman's right to access abortion.

Texas, however, is a predominantly Christian state, with more than half of Texans identifying as belonging to a congregation (rather than just being Christian by birth, for example). Since 1980, Texas has voted Republican in every presidential election. It is perhaps not surprising, therefore, that abortion is a controversial issue in the state, as can be seen in Figure 1.1.

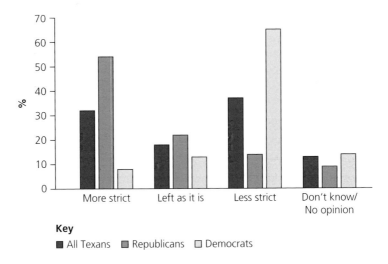

Key
■ All Texans ■ Republicans □ Democrats

Figure 1.1 Opinion polling of Texans' views on abortion restrictions

Source: University of Texas/*Texas Tribune*, 2 March 2021

Over the last 10 years, the restrictions on abortion in Texas have become increasingly strict (see Box 1.1). Funding has been removed from family planning schemes and restrictions have been placed on who can get abortions and what they must go through in order to get one. This had already been the subject of a federal-level Supreme Court case in 2016, which Texas lost. However, in 2021 the Texas legislature passed a law that was the most restrictive anywhere in the USA.

Box 1.1 Timeline of abortion rights in Texas

- September 2011: Texas cuts the family planning budget by two-thirds.
- January 2013: Texas requires a sonogram before abortions.
- July 2013: Texas law HB2 bans abortion after 20 weeks. It also gives doctors the right to admit patients to a local hospital and states that abortion centres must meet surgical standards — both of these are later challenged at the Supreme Court.
- June 2016: the Supreme Court strikes down these two elements of HB2 as unconstitutional.
- June 2017: Texas law SB8 requires foetal tissue to be buried or cremated — this is later blocked by the district court.
- June 2019: Texas law SB24 requires abortion patients to receive a hard copy of *A Woman's Right to Know*, which contains inaccurate information about abortion risks.
- September 2019: Texas doubles funding for the 'Alternatives to Abortion Program'.
- March 2020: an executive order from the governor of Texas bans all 'not medically necessary' abortions due to the Covid-19 pandemic.
- May 2021: Texas law SB8 prohibits abortion after a foetal heartbeat is detected, usually around 6 weeks.

The law, Senate Bill 8 (SB8), makes it all but illegal to have an abortion once a foetal heartbeat has been detected, which usually occurs around the 6-week mark. At this stage of pregnancy, it is not uncommon for a woman not yet to know she is pregnant, making it even more difficult to have an abortion in Texas. The Supreme Court was petitioned for an emergency injunction against the law, which it denied, allowing the law to come into force on 1 September. The law also allowed for private citizens to sue anyone involved in obtaining an abortion and to be awarded $10,000 for successfully doing so. Therefore, family members who might take a woman to an abortion, as well as the woman herself, were a target of the law.

While President Biden described this law as an 'unprecedented assault' on women's rights, the law was able to pass because the state had the power to do so. This highlights the sovereignty of states — that even in the face of explicit criticism from the federal government, they can act as they wish over policy areas that they control. This has not prevented the federal government from trying to take further action. President Biden has ordered his Justice Department to launch a court case against Texas over the law. However, this serves only to demonstrate further the balance of power between states and the federal government. The only way Biden might be able to get Texas to do what he would like is to use constitutional methods. He cannot simply dictate to the states, even when they are enacting highly restrictive laws. The issue of abortion rules in the state of Mississippi was heard at the Supreme Court on the 1 December 2021 in the case of *Dobbs* v. *Jackson Womens' Health Organization*. The result of this case is likely to have wide-reaching impact for the right of US states to restrict abortion.

The growing 'legalisation' of marijuana

While the latest restrictions on abortion in Texas have been swift and severe, the changes to the status of marijuana highlight a more incremental aspect of federalism. Technically, marijuana remains illegal in the USA. Under the Controlled Substances Act 1970, marijuana is a Class I substance, in the same category as heroin. However, since 1996 numerous states have 'legalised' marijuana both medically and/or recreationally. What this has meant in reality is that states have said they are not willing to commit resources to enforcing a federal law. Therefore, if the federal government wants to enforce the law, it will have to use its own resources.

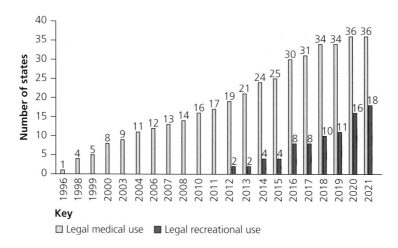

Key
☐ Legal medical use   ■ Legal recreational use

Figure 1.2 States with legalised marijuana use

Often, marijuana has been legalised through ballot initiatives. These are a form of referendum that take place at the same time as a national election, usually the midterms or the presidential election. In 2020, it was notable that there was a significant jump in the number of states that had recreational marijuana on the ballot. This was especially notable as, under President Trump, the Justice Department had said it was going to take a harder line on the use of marijuana in the USA. Therefore, these states were going directly against the policy of the federal government.

Table 1.1 Marijuana on the ballot in 2020

State	Details	Outcome
Arizona	Legalise recreational marijuana for those aged over 21	60% approved
Montana	• Amend the Montana constitution to set a minimum age for marijuana use	58% approved
	• Legalise recreational marijuana for those aged over 21	57% approved
New Jersey	Amend the New Jersey constitution to legalise recreational marijuana for those aged over 21	67% approved
South Dakota	• Amend the South Dakota constitution to legalise recreational marijuana	54% approved*
	• Legalise medical marijuana	70% approved

*later overturned in the courts

Source: Ballotpedia

In all four states that balloted on the issue, the use of recreational marijuana was passed. This was especially notable as two of these states voted for Donald Trump in the 2020 presidential election, supporting him nationally but challenging him through their state policy. This highlights the delicate relationship between the states and federal government, where states are willing to assert their own power against federal law, even when their preferred candidate supports the law.

Table 1.1 shows the creeping trend towards the power of the states in this area over the last three decades, irrespective of the policy beliefs of the federal government. The Obama and Biden administrations have been far less willing to oppose the use of marijuana, but Figure 1.2 suggests the view of the federal government has been irrelevant anyway — the trend towards greater legalisation has continued regardless.

The issue of DC statehood

The importance of the power of the individual states is also seen through the desire of some areas to become a state. In 2017, the people of the US territory of Puerto Rico voted in a referendum that they would like to become the 51st state. Following the events of 6 January 2021 (see Chapter 8), the people of the District of Columbia reiterated their own desire to become the 51st state. In fact, the events were so momentous that the mayor of DC made a statement that very same day (see Box 1.2).

> **Box 1.2** **Excerpt from a statement by Washington DC mayor, Muriel Bowser, 6 January 2021**
>
> Washingtonians have waited over 200 years for the representation we deserve as American citizens. And it is not just the residents of DC who bear the burden of our disenfranchisement. To paraphrase Dr. King: when any American is denied democracy, our entire nation is denied those voices and votes. But now, we are ready to finally fix this injustice by getting statehood on President Biden's desk within the first 100 days of the 117th Congress...we are ready to build a more perfect union...one in which the 712,000 residents of Washington, DC have full access to our nation's democracy.

The issue of statehood for DC is one that anyone who visits the district will be confronted with. The DC number plates all have a statement underneath them that reads 'Taxation without Representation'. This refers to the slogan 'No taxation without representation' used during the Boston Tea Party of 1773, when the British colonies rebelled against the taxes that they were being charged without being represented in the UK Parliament. For DC residents today, it reflects the fact that they pay taxes but have no voting member of Congress.

This is especially acute as DC has a population that is bigger than two other US states and only just smaller than four more (see Table 1.2). There are significant benefits to being recognised as a state. For example, DC currently has no control over its budget, which is set by Congress, and far more limited power than the states to control its own laws and law enforcement agencies.

Table 1.2 Population of states, 2021

State	Population	People per square mile
Wyoming	581,075	6
Vermont	623,251	67
District of Columbia*	714,153	11,011
Alaska	724,357	1
North Dakota	770,026	10
South Dakota	896,581	11
Delaware	990,334	485

*not currently a state

The Biden administration also leant its support to statehood for the District of Columbia (see Box 1.3). This perhaps suggests that the relationship between states and the federal government is not always as tense as some of the other examples in this chapter suggest. The White House statement also represents how important the principles of the US Constitution remain today, both in terms of federalism but also in advancing the principle of democracy.

Box 1.3 **Excerpt from White House Statement of Administration Policy on HR51, Washington, DC Admission Act**

The Administration strongly supports H.R. 51, the Washington, D.C. Admission Act. For far too long, the more than 700,000 people of Washington, D.C. have been deprived of full representation in the U.S. Congress. This taxation without representation and denial of self-governance is an affront to the democratic values on which our Nation was founded. H.R. 51 rights this wrong by making Washington, D.C. a state and providing its residents with long overdue full representation in Congress.

Following these developments, a bill was introduced to Congress to make Washington DC a state. In April 2021 the bill passed the House of Representatives, but it must also be passed by the Senate and signed by the president before it can be enacted. No action took place on the bill between April and October 2021.

Federalism when crises occur

The insurrection of 6 January 2021, described in Chapter 8, was not the only crisis to occur during the year. The principle of federalism is often placed under particular strain during times of crisis — states often want to be able to exercise their power and control the response to a crisis, but do not always have the means to do so. Hurricane Ida caused a huge swathe of damage through the USA in the summer of 2021, but most notably in Louisiana. This was the same state that had been hit in 2005 by Hurricane Katrina and it was better prepared this time. Nonetheless, the cost of the damage was significant.

The cost of such natural disasters often far exceeds states' ability to afford it themselves. In Louisiana, the total state revenue is $36.1 billion but the estimated damage from Hurricane Ida was $70–80 billion. In such situations, states often rely on the federal government to step in and help out. In the case of Hurricane Ida, the federal government supported with money, resources and even the army. Therefore, it is clear that despite some areas of increasing state power, there comes a point where ultimately they rely upon their relationship with the much larger and therefore better resourced federal government.

However, the federal government cannot just enforce its views or assistance upon states during crises. States remain sovereign and therefore sometimes the federal government must await a request from a state governor for assistance. This was seen very clearly through President Biden's statement following the unexpected collapse of a Miami building in June 2021 (see Box 1.4), with Biden seeming to implore the state of Florida to request federal assistance.

> **Box 1.4** **President Biden comments on the building collapse in Miami**
>
> President Joe Biden said he was waiting for Mr DeSantis to declare an emergency and officials from the Federal Emergency Management Agency (Fema) were already at the scene.
>
> 'I say to the people of Florida, whatever help you want, what the federal government can provide, we're waiting, just ask us. We'll be there.'
>
> Source: BBC News, 25 June 2021

The reaction of states and federal government in a crisis is a very useful lens through which to examine the relationships in federalism. It can demonstrate the dependence of states on federal government in the event of mass disaster, and yet a determination of states to maintain their own sovereignty and carry out their own response. As crises are often unpredictable, this helps to explain why the power balance between federal and state government can change so frequently.

The 2020 census

Perhaps one of the key events that can help to explain why different states view the federal government so differently is the census. The census takes place every 10 years, asking for details about all citizens in the USA, including their gender, religion and ethnicity. The resulting data help to show the vast differences that exist between the states, which may help to explain their differing opinions. Figure 1.3 shows the ethnic breakdown of a number of states in 2019. The huge difference between the states can help to explain why some of them experienced a backlash when they tried to pass voter ID laws in 2020/21 that have been seen as targeting minority ethnic communities.

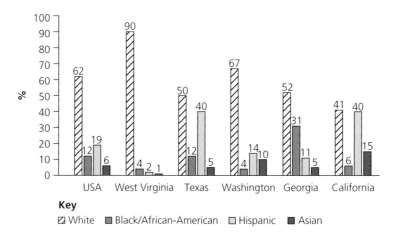

Key
White ■ Black/African-American □ Hispanic ■ Asian

Figure 1.3 Ethnicity by state, 2019

Source: US Census Bureau

Note: the Texas and California figures add up to more than 100%. This is because the Census Bureau records being Hispanic as a background and the other characteristics here as 'race'.

The other crucial result of the census is a redistribution of seats in the House of Representatives to reflect changes in the populations of states. Those states from which people have moved will lose seats, while those states which have increased in population will gain seats. This can have a huge impact on the party make-up of the House of Representatives, but it also affects how many Electoral College votes a state receives in the presidential election.

The results of the 2020 census mean that in the next election, the states that voted for Biden in the 2020 election will be worth three fewer votes, while the states that voted for Trump will be worth three more (see Table 1.3). Obviously, it cannot be guaranteed how these states will vote in 2024, but these changes could have an impact on the presidential election result.

Table 1.3 Changes to House of Representatives seats following 2020 census

States that lost a seat	States that gained a seat	States that gained two seats
California (54)	North Carolina (16)	Texas (40)
Pennsylvania (19)	Oregon (8)	
Ohio (17)	Colorado (10)	
Illinois (19)	Montana (4)	
New York (28)	Florida (30)	
Michigan (15)		
West Virginia (4)		

Source: NPR

Comparison

- Federalism in the USA means that states have considerably more guaranteed power than the UK devolved bodies. Sovereignty is guaranteed to the states by the US Constitution, whereas the UK devolved bodies, at least in theory, exist only because the UK Parliament allows them to, and could be closed down and withdrawn by a new parliamentary statute.
- The reality of life for citizens, however, is more similar. In both the USA and the UK, the daily life of citizens can be more affected by their state/devolved government than by federal government. For example, the rules implemented in response to Covid-19 were different between states across the USA and between devolved bodies in the UK. In both cases, these differences led to conflict between regional governments and the national government.
- The nature of the division of powers in the USA and UK is also similar. The US Constitution guarantees that the federal government has some powers while the states have others. In the UK, these are called reserved matters and devolved matters. Reserved matters remain with the government at Westminster, such as foreign policy, while devolved matters are given to the regions to make policy upon, such as the varied response to Covid-19 by the UK devolved governments.

Summary

- The relationship between the federal government and state governments in the USA has always been fragile and changeable. However, in recent years, the controversy for some states of the Obama and Trump administrations has meant that states have been increasingly asserting their own power.
- The relationship between the states and federal government varies depending on the issue, and this is not always as predictable as might be expected. While it is possible to assume Texas might be against abortion, the number of states that are increasingly in favour of legalising marijuana, regardless of their majority political persuasion, is perhaps more surprising.
- The national circumstances are crucial when evaluating the condition of federalism in the USA today. States are often ill-equipped to deal with natural disasters or other unexpected crises, and therefore may rely on federal government for aid at these times.
- The federal government can try and apply pressure to states, but their avenues to do this are limited by the US Constitution. Presidential pressure may be applied through statements or funding to try and bring a state around to the government's way of thinking.
- The census which occurs every 10 years can be used to explain some of the vast differences that exist between states due to the make-up of their state population.

Further reading and research

- Read 'South Carolina court halts executions until firing squad is available' (bbc.co.uk, 17 June 2021). How can this example be used to support the power of states in the USA?
- Read '9th Circuit Appeals Court blocks the overturn of California's assault weapons ban' (edition.cnn.com, 22 June 2021). What does this example suggest might be limits on the state's power to make its own law?
- Read 'Attacking anti-vaccine movement, Biden mandates widespread COVID shots, tests' (reuters.com, 10 September 2021). What does this article suggest about the power, or lack of power, the federal government has over states?
- Read 'Federalism failing to meet 21st century needs' (theday.com, 28 February 2021). Do you believe that federalism is appropriate for twenty-first-century America?

Chapter 2

Representation in the 117th Congress

Context

- Representation is one of the most important functions of Congress and can take many forms.
- Congress should also act as a microcosm of the USA. It should be functionally representative (representing various social and economic groups) and descriptively representative (representing the electorate in terms of characteristics such as age, gender, ethnicity and religion) to ensure all voters are fairly and effectively represented, irrespective of state or district lines. This is important in a representative democracy.
- Members of the House of Representatives, who are elected every 2 years, and senators, who are elected every 6 years, should represent their constituents in Congress. Although members can be defeated through challenges in primaries and caucuses, the incumbency rates in both the House and the Senate remain high (93% overall in 2020).
- Members of Congress can use earmarks to 'bring home the bacon' for their constituents, earmarking funds for local projects by adding provisions to appropriations bills. Funds directed to unnecessary projects in a state or district are known as 'pork barrel' spending. Earmarks were reintroduced in 2021 and have been used by members of the 117th Congress to fund projects in their local state or district.
- Redistricting takes place after the national census every 10 years (the last one was in 2020), and is used to redraw the 435 district boundaries. It is done by the party in control of the state's legislature, and therefore is open to political manipulation. The manipulation of redistricting to secure a favourable political outcome for one party is known as gerrymandering. This affects representation negatively in Congress, as it leads to unequal political representation and can lead to many wasted votes. Districts that are not fair and competitive are arguably a hindrance to democracy.

Exam success

AQA	3.2.1.2	The legislative branch of government: Congress
		Representative role of senators and representatives
Edexcel	2.2	The functions of Congress
	2.2.1	Representation
	5	US democracy and participation

For the Edexcel specification you need to understand the representative function of Congress, including congressional elections and the significance of incumbency. The high incumbency rates in Congress can be attributed to many factors. The changes to earmarking in 2021 and redistricting will be important contributing factors to incumbency in the 2022 midterm elections. Most importantly, you need to appreciate the debates about the adequacy of Congress's representative role. This might feature on Edexcel Paper 3 Comparative Politics — USA, in section C as a 30-mark essay question or in section A or B as a 12-mark comparative US/UK question.

Similarly, for AQA you need to understand the representative role of senators and House representatives, and debates concerning the functions, powers and effectiveness of Congress. This might feature on AQA Paper 2 Government and Politics of the USA and Comparative Politics, in section A as a 9-mark question, in section B as a 25-mark extract question or in section C as a 25-mark comparative US/UK essay question on the functions of the legislatures, representation in the USA and UK, or even in relation to a broader question about democracy or political parties.

For either board, being able to evaluate the extent to which Congress performs representation effectively, and having an awareness of recent changes that make Congress either more or less effective with regard to representation, is crucial to exam success. You need recent examples of members of Congress representing their constituents and an appreciation of recent changes, including the reintroduction of earmarking, changes to district boundaries following redistricting, and figures revealing the social composition of the current Congress. It is important to know which particular groups are most under- and over-represented in Congress and how this can impact on Congress's ability effectively to fulfil not just its function of representation but also its functions of legislation and oversight.

Representation can be brought into several exam questions relating to the overall effectiveness of Congress as well as other questions relating to democracy, elections and parties. If Congress is unrepresentative, this can impact on the extent to which the US political system continues to be a beacon of democracy. This in turn can be linked to other topics such as the electoral system and political parties. Hyper-partisanship has led to a situation in which the party has become a more important factor than constituents for many representatives when voting in Congress. The ability to evaluate representation in Congress successfully will enable you to evaluate the changing role of parties in the US system of government, divisions within and between these parties, and the extent to which the US political system as a whole works. You also need to be able to compare the extent to which Congress performs its representative and other functions better than the UK Parliament.

Earmarking and representation in Congress

Changes to earmarking in 2021

Earmarking is a way for members of Congress to add amendments to appropriations bills, in order to grant funds to their district or state for specific projects or programmes, rather than allowing federal officials to use a merit-based system or a formula to decide how to spend the money granted by Congress to a certain area. This change has an important impact on representation in the 117th Congress.

In 2021 both the Democrats and the Republicans reintroduced earmarking in the House of Representatives. Earmarking had been banned since the 112th Congress in 2011 due to accusations that it led to wasteful spending, corruption scandals linked to lobbyists attempting to bribe representatives to include earmarks benefiting them, and members only supporting bills if their state or district benefited, which often ignored more important projects.

Why is earmarking important for representation?

Earmarking can improve representation because members of Congress are able to use their knowledge of the local community in their district or state to direct the funds to where they are most needed, allowing members to be more responsive to the people. Representatives are in a better position to do this than a federal official because members of Congress are in close contact with their constituents and can therefore be advised where the funds are best placed. While this may be true, it can lead to wasteful spending (pork barrel) and an increased pressure to please local voters rather than considering the whole country. Also, certain individuals are more successful than others in achieving earmarking to benefit their state or district, which does not improve the representation for all. Individuals who are members of the House of Representatives and Senate Appropriations Committees are in the best position to do this successfully.

The Democrats in the House of Representatives sought to address this issue by attaching strict transparency and accountability rules to earmarking, including not allowing requests that would benefit themselves or their family members financially. In addition, all members of the House of Representatives were able to make up to 10 requests each for 'Community Project Funding' for their state or district.

While Republicans in the House voted 102–84 by secret ballot in March 2021 to participate, effectively overturning their 2011 ban on earmarking, Republican senators in April 2021 opted not to. The return of earmarking was criticised by fiscally conservative Republicans in the House Freedom Caucus for being a wasteful use of funds.

Earmarking and the Democrats' changes to it are important when considering oversight in Congress as well as representation. The changes that the Democrats made to the process of earmarking have aided representation in Congress, as they prevent a small number of individuals who sit on the Appropriations Committees from being able to unfairly dominate and take advantage of earmarking, and they allow members to channel funds directly where they are most needed in their district or state. This is also important when evaluating how democratic the US system of government is. Although it may appear to be undemocratic to reintroduce earmarking, the added transparency and fairness of the new system means that it is more democratic than it was in the past and requests can be more easily scrutinised. This is important when considering Congress's oversight function. It reminds us that members of Congress are not just tasked with overseeing the actions of the executive branch, but also with scrutinising each other.

However, earmarking arguably damages Congress's legislative function and can encourage bills to be passed only if they contain enough earmarks to secure the necessary votes. This is all-important when considering how effectively Congress performs its functions: Congress's representative function may be more effective as a result of the reintroduction of earmarking, but it might mean that it performs its legislative function less effectively.

A check on executive power

The constitution states that Congress can decide how much money the federal government can spend as well as where this money is spent. It could therefore be argued that the return of earmarking allows Congress to fulfil its appropriations function more effectively.

During the ban on earmarking, Congress's constitutional authority to direct how money is expended through the 'power of the purse' was essentially delegated to the executive branch. This is important when considering presidential power. Without earmarking in Congress, the executive branch assumes even more power than the Founding Fathers intended because federal officials in the executive branch are responsible for appropriating funds rather than Congress. These officials are susceptible to pressure from the president or lobbying from individuals in Congress via lettermarking (see Box 2.1).

Box 2.1   What is lettermarking?

Appropriations bills sometimes include funds for projects not requested by the executive branch. This allow members of Congress to 'lettermark' these funds by unofficially contacting executive officials directly and requesting that the funds are directed to their state or district.

Therefore, understanding earmarking can be useful when considering how checks and balances have been enhanced in recent years through the changes introduced by the House Democrats. This process aids transparency and prevents the president and the executive branch from having too much influence over the power of the purse.

An example of Community Project Funding

R. M. Keating Historical Enterprise Park in Middletown, Connecticut, received $1 million in Community Project Funding in August 2021 to renovate and modernise a former industrial building into usable spaces for small non-profit businesses and community events. Middletown is in Connecticut's 3rd congressional district and its representative is Democrat chair of the House Appropriations Committee, Rosa DeLauro. The project was one of seven government spending bills, which included earmarks through Community Project Funding, passed in July 2021. The seven appropriations bills passed by 219–208 votes.

This example reveals that the changes introduced by the Democrats failed to prevent individuals who sit on the Appropriations Committees from benefiting the most. It is also a useful example to include when evaluating the power of committee chairs and allows us to question whether all members of Congress can perform their representative function equally and adequately. Finally, the close vote reiterates the partisanship that continues to exist in the 117th Congress.

Redistricting and representation in Congress in 2021

Changes to district boundaries in 2021

In 2021 the Census Bureau announced that seven seats in the House of Representatives will change because of the 2020 census. The states that will lose and gain seats are shown in Tables 2.1 and 2.2.

Table 2.1 States that will gain seats

State	Change	Party in control of the state legislature	Change in population since 2010 census (%)
Texas	+2	Republican	+15.5
Colorado	+1	Democrat	+14.6
Florida	+1	Republican	+14.1
Montana	+1	Republican	+9.2
North Carolina	+1	Republican	+9.3
Oregon	+1	Democrat	+10.2

Source: USA Today

Table 2.2 States that will lose seats

State	Change	Party in control of the state legislature	Change in population since 2010 census (%)
California	−1	Democrat	+6.0
Illinois	−1	Democrat	−0.3
Michigan	−1	Republican	+1.7
New York	−1	Democrat	+4.1
Ohio	−1	Republican	+2.1
Pennsylvania	−1	Republican	+2.2
West Virginia	−1	Republican	−3.5

Source: USA Today

Why is this significant?

- The Democrats have a majority of only six in the House of Representatives. However, this majority will increase to seven once Troy Carter officially replaces Cedric Richmond, who joined the executive branch as the director of the White House Office of Public Engagement.
- The Republicans could take control of the House of Representatives in 2022 if a few seats flip from Democrat to Republican in the midterm elections.

- The states that will gain seats tend to be Republican-leaning states whereas the states that will lose seats tend to be Democrat leaning.
- Montana gained a representative, so it now has two representatives, each representing 542,704 residents. This means that Montana's House members represent the fewest people. Delaware's sole representative represents the most people, 990,837.
- The US population has increased by 7.4% since the last census in 2010. California's population of 39,538,223 means that its senators represent the largest number of people each, 19,769,112, whereas Wyoming's senators represent the fewest people, 288,426, as its population is only 576,851.
- As states are responsible for redrawing the district boundaries to accommodate the changes, gerrymandering (the manipulation of an electoral constituency boundary to benefit one party) could be used by the state legislature.
- Republicans currently control redistricting in 20 states, which contain 187 congressional districts, whereas the Democrats control 8 states, which contain 75 congressional districts. If the Republican state legislatures engage in gerrymandering in 2022, it could be challenged in the Supreme Court.
- The process is fairer in the states that are not controlled by one political party or that choose to allow an independent redistricting committee to draw their boundaries. However, only 10 states currently opt to use independent commissions to draw district lines. In 6 states, the Republicans and Democrats each control one chamber in the state legislature, which means that neither can dominate the redistricting process.
- The Republican Party controls the state legislatures in 8 out of the 13 states that will see a change to the number of seats they have in the 2022 midterm elections. This provides the Republicans with more opportunity to maximise the changes to their advantage, and to determine who controls Congress in 2022.
- The decline of the white non-Hispanic population to 57.8%, revealed in the 2020 census, could damage the Republican vote as white non-Hispanic voters are more likely to vote Democrat than Republican. However, this is unlikely to dilute the influence that the Republicans can exercise over redistricting ahead of the 2022 midterm elections.
- The Democrats have attempted to ban partisan gerrymandering through the 'For the People Act'. It passed in the House of Representatives by 220–210 in March 2021 but failed to pass in the Senate in June 2021 after opposition from Republican senators via the filibuster. The bill would have required states to use independent commissions to draw congressional district maps and adopt automatic voter registration.

This is useful when evaluating the extent to which the US political system is democratic and effective. Gerrymandering affects representation in Congress negatively, as it leads to unequal political representation and potentially to many wasted votes. It is ultimately undemocratic.

How diverse is the 117th Congress?

As mentioned in the context box (page 15), it is important for elected members to be functionally and descriptively representative in a representative democracy. We will look at diversity in terms of ethnicity, gender, age and religion.

Ethnicity

The 117th Congress is the most racially and ethnically diverse in history (see Table 2.3), with 124 members of the House of Representatives and the Senate identifying as black, Hispanic, Asian-American, or Native American, which accounts for 23% of congressional members. This is significant because it represents a 97% increase in 20 years. However, Democrats account for 83% of the current racial and ethnic minorities in Congress compared with the Republicans' 17%. Moreover, non-Hispanic white Americans remain over-represented in Congress: 77% of members of the current Congress are non-Hispanic white Americans whereas the 2020 census revealed that only 58% of the US population is.

Table 2.3 Number of black, Hispanic, Asian-American, and Native American members of Congress, 2001–21

Congress	Black	Hispanic	Asian-American	Native American
107th (2001)	36	19	7	1
108th (2003)	37	22	6	2
109th (2005)	41	25	7	1
110th (2007)	41	26	8	1
111th (2009)	39	26	7	1
112th (2011)	42	29	10	1
113th (2013)	42	31	11	2
114th (2015)	46	32	11	2
115th (2017)	50	39	15	2
116th (2019)	56	43	17	4
117th (2021)	59	46	17	6

Note: The figures for the 117th Congress add up to 128 because some of the 124 members identify as more than one ethnicity.

Source: Pew Research

House of Representatives

Black, Hispanic, Asian-American and Native Americans make up 26% of the House. 13% of members of the House are Black, which is similar to the US population overall. 1% of members of the House identify as Native American, which is again is similar to the US population overall.

Four members of the House of Representatives identify under more than one racial or ethnic identity (see Table 2.4).

Table 2.4 House of Representatives members identifying under more than racial or ethnic identity

Name	Party	District		
Bobby Scott	Democrat	VA-3	Black	Asian
Antonio Delgado	Democrat	NY-19	Black	Hispanic
Ritchie Torres	Democrat	NY-15	Black	Hispanic
Marilyn Strickland	Democrat	WA-10	Black	Asian

Despite Kai Kahele (D-HI-2) identifying as both Native American and Portuguese American, he is only listed as Native American and not Hispanic because Portuguese-Americans are not included in the Hispanic figures.

Senate

Eleven Senators identify as a racial or ethnic minority in the 117th Congress compared with nine in the previous Congress.

Table 2.5 Members identifying as a racial or ethnic minority

Name	Party	State	Race/Ethnicity	First elected
Bob Menendez	Democrat	New Jersey	Hispanic	2006
Marco Rubio	Republican	Florida	Hispanic	2011
Mazie Hirono	Democrat	Hawaii	Asian-American	2013
Ted Cruz	Republican	Texas	Hispanic	2013
Tim Scott	Republican	South Carolina	Black	2013
Cory Booker	Democrat	New Jersey	Black	2013
Tammy Duckworth	Democrat	Illinois	Asian-American	2017
Catherine Cortez Masto	Democrat	Nevada	Hispanic	2017
Ben Ray Lujan	Democrat	New Mexico	Hispanic	2021
Raphael Warnock	Democrat	Georgia	Black	2021
Alex Padilla	Democrat	California	Hispanic	2021

Raphael Warnock became the first Black Senator to represent Georgia and Alex Padilla became the first Hispanic Senator to represent California. In the 232-year history of the US Senate, only 11 Senators have been Black.

This is important when considering increased racial tensions in the USA in recent years relating to the death of George Floyd and the increased prevalence of the Black Lives Matter movement. Race has always been an important factor in US politics, so having the most racially and ethnically diverse Congress in history matters.

The racial composition of Congress can be useful when evaluating race and the protection of rights in the USA as well as differences between the parties on these issues.

Gender

The 117th Congress is the most representative in history when looking at the number of women representatives. However, despite the significant increase in women in Congress, they remain one of the most under-represented groups with only 27% of representatives as compared to 51% of the US population (see Table 2.6).

Table 2.6 Number of women in the 117th Congress

	Number of representatives	Proportion of Congress (%)
House of Representatives	120	27
Senate	24	24
Congress overall	144	27

Source: Pew Research

Age

The increase in the proportion of younger members in the House of Representatives was not as pronounced in the 117th Congress as it had been in the previous Congress (see Table 2.7).

Table 2.7 Proportion of House representatives from each generation (%)

Generation	115th Congress	116th Congress	117th Congress
Silent (born 1928–45)	10	9	6
Boomer (born 1946–64)	62	54	53
Generation X (born 1965–80)	27	32	33
Millennial (born 1981–96)	1	6	7

Source: Pew Research

Jon Ossoff (D-GA) became the first Millennial senator at the age of 33 in January 2021 and the number of Generation X senators increased from 16 in the 115th Congress to 20 in the 117th Congress (see Table 2.8).

Table 2.8 Proportion of senators from each generation (%)

Generation	115th Congress	116th Congress	117th Congress
Silent (born 1928–45)	19	15	11
Boomer (born 1946–64)	65	66	68
Generation X (born 1965–80)	16	19	20
Millennial (born 1981–96)	0	0	1

Source: Pew Research

Religion

The current Congress contains the fewest Christians since 1961. However, Christians are still vastly over-represented in Congress compared to the US population: 88% of members of the 117th Congress are Christian compared with 65% of the US electorate (see Table 2.9).

Table 2.9 Christians in the 117th Congress

	Number in Congress	% of Congress	% of US adults
Protestant	294	55.4	43
Catholic	158	29.8	20
Mormon	9	1.7	2
Orthodox Christian	7	1.3	<1
Total Christians	468	88.1	65

Source: Pew Research

It may appear that Congress is not very religiously diverse, especially when looking at non-Christian groups. However, when you compare the figures to the US population, Congress is revealed as being more representative than first appears (see Table 2.10). The most over-represented non-Christian group are Jewish members of Congress, who account for 6.2% of seats in the House of Representatives and the Senate but only 2% of the US population overall. Only two non-Christian members of Congress are Republicans; both are Jewish. The only Buddhist, Muslim, Hindu, and unaffiliated members of Congress are Democrats. However, it is important to note that while members of Congress may identify as having a specific religion, they may not be practising that religion but may choose to identify with it to win votes.

Table 2.10 Non-Christians in the 117th Congress

	Number in Congress	% of Congress	% of US adults
Jewish	33	6.2	2
Buddhist	2	0.4	1
Muslim	3	0.6	1
Hindu	2	0.4	1
Unitarian Universalist	3	0.6	<1
Unaffiliated	1	0.2	26
Other	1	0.2	3
Don't know	18	3.4	2

Source: Pew Research

The group most under-represented in Congress are those with no religious affiliation. The only member of Congress who says that she is atheist, agnostic or nothing is Senator Kyrsten Sinema (D-AZ), who states that she is religiously unaffiliated. This is compared with 26% of the US population who are either atheist, agnostic or religiously unaffiliated. This means that there are no representatives in the House representing the 26% of the US population who are not religious.

Congress remains religiously significantly unrepresentative of the US population but has become slightly more diverse in recent years. This is important when evaluating the extent to which Congress is effective in relation to its representative function, and the extent to which the US is an effective (representative) democracy. The differences between representatives from the Democrat and Republican parties is useful when evaluating differences between the parties and factors that affect electoral outcomes; the number of representatives from each group that each party has may explain why certain groups are more likely to vote for certain parties.

Case study: Lisa Murkowski and representation

- Despite being a Republican senator for Alaska, Murkowski offered support to, and was a key negotiator of, Biden's 2021 Infrastructure Investment and Jobs Act. Through this, Murkowski was able to secure significant funding for Alaskan infrastructure projects, including $3.5 billion for roads and $225 million for bridges. Murkowski personally proposed, and secured, $1 billion to support a ferry service, the Alaska Marine Highway System, for local communities.
- In May 2021, Murkowski persuaded President Biden to approve Project Willow, an oil-drilling project in Alaska's National Petroleum Reserve, despite significant opposition from Democrats.
- Murkowski faced criticism for failing to persuade Biden not to suspend oil drilling licences in the Arctic National Wildlife Refuge, which the Native American group Inupiat, including 13,500 Inuit people, rely on.
- In March 2021 the Alaska Republican Party voted to distance itself from Murkowski, after she failed to support Trump's American Healthcare Act in 2017, claiming that it would be even worse than the current Act for many Alaskans, and voted to impeach Trump in February 2021.
- Murkowski is likely to face a primary challenge in 2022 but was endorsed for re-election by the Senate Leadership Committee, which is run by allies of the Senate minority leader, Mitch McConnell. The committee, which is a political funding organisation, has raised twice as much money as Murkowski's rivals.
- Murkowski may benefit from changes passed by Alaska in Ballot Measure 2 in November 2020. From 2022 the old party primaries will be replaced by a single non-partisan primary that reduces the contenders down to four individuals, whom voters then vote for in a rank order preference. Murkowski is highly likely to be one of the final four and should benefit from the rank order system, as more than half of Alaskan voters are not affiliated to a particular political party.

How to use this case study in your exams

- These examples highlight the difficulty that representatives face with regard to representation. Murkowski's moderate position is representative of most Alaskans who are not party affiliated, but she faces pressure from within her own party to represent the views of the Republican Party, the party that she represents.

- It is important to remember that representatives cannot represent everybody. However, Murkowski faced significant criticism for failing to represent two key groups: members of the Republican Party, by voting against the American Healthcare Act and in favour of impeaching Trump; and Native Americans, who had their oil licences in the far north of Alaska suspended. This is a useful example of minority groups failing to be represented adequately in Congress and the difficulty that representatives face when trying to balance the views of their party and constituents.

- Murkowski's willingness to work with Biden in exchange for benefits for Alaska is useful when studying presidential power. It reveals the importance of presidential persuasion as an informal presidential power and reiterates that the president needs to persuade not only members of their own party to support their legislation in Congress, but quite often members of the other party, especially in the Senate when 60 votes are often needed to avoid the filibuster. It is also a good example of bipartisanship as well as being useful when looking at limitations on presidential power: Biden had to go against his own party and its climate change agenda to support Project Willow, but this was necessary to get Murkowski's support for other things. It highlights constraints placed on a president, even when their party controls Congress and they are in their first term, as the filibuster threat in the Senate means that presidents need to rely on some senators from the other party to support their agenda.

- Murkowski's willingness to break ranks with her own party during an era of heightened hyper-partisanship is useful when studying parties, as it shows that there are still some moderate representatives who do not simply vote in a partisan way on every issue. However, the criticism that Murkowski faced from her own party in March 2021 is a useful example of the increasing power and dominance of parties in US politics and the difficulty that representatives have in representing the views of some of their constituents if they go against the position taken by the party.

- Ballot Measure 2, which was passed in 2020 and will come into force in 2022, is a useful example when answering questions about elections, and particularly primaries, as it illustrates the different rules that states have and the impact this has on incumbency.

- The Senate Leadership Committee is a useful example when studying elections and parties, as it reveals the importance of funding and receiving support from the party leadership in Congress when incumbents are seeking re-election, due to the possibility of a primary challenge.

Comparison

It is important to look at similarities and differences when answering exam questions about how effectively Congress and the UK Parliament fulfil their representative function.

Differences

- The district boundaries in the House of Representatives are redrawn every 10 years, unlike in the UK where the independent Boundary Commission reviews boundaries every 5 years and suggests changes. There have not been any changes in the UK since 2010 but the current government is trying to pass legislation that will lead to boundary changes. In 2022, Texas will gain two extra representatives. Gerrymandering can occur because most district boundaries are redrawn by the party controlling the state legislature, unlike in the UK. The Republican Party will decide 8 out of 13 district changes in 2022.
- Members of Congress can be unseated in primary challenges, unlike MPs. Lisa Murkowski (R-AK) is likely to face a primary challenge in Alaska in 2022.
- Earmarks can be added to appropriations bills in the USA to direct funds to community projects in a representative's district or state, unlike in the UK. Rosa DeLauro (CT-3) secured funding for a project in Middletown, Connecticut, in her district.

Similarities

- In both the USA and UK, members must balance pressure to vote with their party and the interests of their constituents. Lisa Murkowski represents many moderates in her state of Alaska but faces criticism for not always voting with the Republican Party.
- There are many safe seats in both the USA and the UK and a high incumbency rate in both legislatures: 93% of Congress was re-elected in 2020 compared with 76% of MPs in 2019.
- Both Congress and Parliament have become more descriptively representative in recent years. The 117th Congress is the most racially and ethnically diverse so far and contains the highest number of women of any Congress. The current Parliament is also the most diverse in history with 34% of MPs women and 10% of MPs being from a non-white background.

Summary

- The reintroduction of earmarking in 2021, after a 10-year ban, via 'Community Project Funding' has provided the opportunity for members of Congress to represent their constituents more effectively by directing funds to local projects. However, Republican senators decided not to reintroduce earmarks and many fiscally conservative Republicans in the House of Representatives see them as a wasteful use of funds.
- In 2021 the Census Bureau announced that seven seats in the House of Representatives will change because of the 2020 census. This will impact the outcome of the 2022 midterm elections and is likely to benefit the Republicans more than the Democrats, especially if the Republicans engage in gerrymandering.
- The 117th Congress is the most racially and ethnically diverse ever. It also contains the most women. A total of 23% of congressional members identify as black, Hispanic, Asian-American, or Native American, while 27% of members are women. There is only one non-affiliated or non-religious member of Congress, compared with 26% of the population — this group are the most under-represented in Congress.
- The party has become an increasingly important factor that representatives must consider when voting in Congress. Lisa Murkowski is likely to face a primary challenge in 2022, but changes made to the Alaskan primary system in 2022 may help her re-election bid.

Further reading and research

- Find out more about women in the 117th Congress by reading *Women in Congress: Statistics and Brief Overview* (**sgp.fas.org**).
- Find out more about the religious make-up of the 117th Congress by reading 'Faith on the Hill: the religious composition of the 117th Congress' (**pewforum.org**).
- Find out what Community Project Funding requests Antonio Delgado (D-NY-19) made in 2021 at: **https://tinyurl.com/3tdzvyu5**
- Find out why Senate Republicans decided not to reintroduce earmarks in 2021, by reading 'Senate Republicans to keep earmark ban, though GOP conference rules offer some wiggle room' (**edition.cnn.com**).

Chapter 3

President Biden's first year

Context

- Joe Biden was sworn in as the 46th US president on 20 January 2021, during a time of great division between the Democrat and Republican parties, most recently because some Republican members of Congress had challenged the validity of the Electoral College's decision.
- In looking at how successful Biden has been so far, we can consider his power of persuasion. Presidents must persuade members of their own party to support their legislative agenda as well as some members from the other party, especially in the Senate when 60 votes out of a possible 100 are often needed to pass a bill, rather than just a simple majority. Biden successfully used his power of persuasion to secure support from 19 Republican senators for the Infrastructure Investment and Jobs Act but struggled to persuade members of his own party to agree on the Budget Reconciliation Bill.
- The deep divisions in Congress will make legislative victories difficult for Biden, even though the Democrats have control of both the House of Representatives and the Senate.
- Presidents can use their implied powers, stated in Article II of the Constitution, to carry out executive action without congressional involvement or oversight. Biden was able to reverse much of Trump's legacy this way. The divisions in Congress mean that Biden will need to rely on this power to advance his agenda, especially in relation to policy issues that deeply divide the two parties, such as immigration, LGBTQ+ rights and the environment.
- The president, as head of state and commander-in-chief, faces fewer constraints in foreign policy than in domestic policy as Congress can place fewer restrictions on the president's actions. Biden was able to make decisions single-handedly about the withdrawal of US troops from Afghanistan but faced much criticism for the decisions he made.

Exam success

AQA	3.2.1.2	The legislative branch of government: Congress
		Relationship of Congress to the executive branch of government
	3.2.1.3	The executive branch of government: president
Edexcel	2.2	The functions of Congress
	2.2.3	Oversight — factors that influence the relationship between Congress and the presidency
	3	US presidency

For the Edexcel specification, you need to:

- Understand the formal sources of presidential power that are outlined in the US Constitution, both as head of state and as head of the government, and how the US president can use these powers. You must be able to use examples from presidents since 1992, including recent examples of how Biden has exercised his powers in comparison to his predecessors.
- Understand the informal sources of presidential power, including the electoral mandate, executive orders, national events and the cabinet, as well as the power of persuasion and other agencies that can act as informal sources of presidential power. Again, you need to be able to use examples since 1992, but the more recent, the better.
- Understand the relationship between the president and Congress, and limitations on presidential power, including Congress and the Constitution. You need to be able to analyse how presidential power changes over time, affected by the president's term in office, the election cycle and divided government.
- Analyse the early stages of a president's time in office, and their power when their party has control of Congress. However, this chapter provides useful illustrations of restrictions on the power of the president even during this time.
- Evaluate how effectively a president has achieved their aims, the debate surrounding the 'imperial presidency', the extent to which the president is held to account by Congress, and the president's power in relation to foreign policy.
- Understand that these debates could all potentially feature as a 30-mark essay question in section C of Edexcel Paper 3 Comparative Politics — USA.

For the AQA specification, you need to:

- Understand the debate about the 'imperial versus imperilled' presidency and the relationship between the president and other institutions, such as the cabinet and agencies.
- Understand the differences between the formal and informal powers of the president, and how the implied powers have been stretched in recent years.
- Evaluate the effectiveness of constraints on presidential power, including the formal system of checks and balances, the party and Congress, as well as the media and public opinion.
- Understand one example of presidential power waxing and waning and have two relevant examples to demonstrate how the sources of presidential power have been used by different presidents. There is no requirement to use examples exclusively from after 1992. However, as with any Politics response, always try to use the most recent relevant examples.
- Understand that these debates could feature on AQA Paper 2 Government and Politics of the USA and Comparative Politics, either in section B as a 25-mark extract question or in section C as a 25-mark comparative US/UK essay question.

The presidency is an important aspect of both specifications and can be used synoptically to evaluate the effectiveness of Congress, particularly its oversight and legislative functions, and the extent to which the US Constitution remains effective (in relation to the expansion of presidential power beyond the Founding Fathers' intentions).

Biden's first 100 days

Joe Biden pledged to use his first 100 days in office to roll back several policies from the Trump era. Biden has made it clear, through the White House Press Secretary, Jen Psaki, that he believes executive action should not be used excessively but can be used to eliminate bad policies that cannot wait. Biden was reluctant to bypass Congress in the way that Trump did, and Obama was forced to after losing control of Congress, but nor did he want to wait for Congress to pass a bill before being able to reverse much of Trump's legacy.

Box 3.1 **Key definitions**

Executive order: an instruction issued by the president to federal officials, which tells them how to carry out Acts passed by Congress. Executive orders are used to make significant changes that affect numerous agencies and departments.

Presidential memorandum: like an executive order, a written instruction from the president to other officials in the executive branch, which tells them how to implement the law. Unlike an executive order, it is not recorded in the Federal Register and given an official number. Presidential memorandums tend to relate to technical aspects of the law.

Proclamation: recorded and numbered, like an executive order, but tends to be an announcement relating to foreign policy matters.

Executive action: refers to all of the above.

Despite Biden's reluctance to use executive action, Tables 3.1–3.3 reveal that he used more executive actions during his first month, and his first 100 days, as president than any president since Roosevelt in 1933. Most of these actions were to reverse his predecessor's policies.

Table 3.1 How do Biden's executive orders compare to previous presidents'?

President	Number of executive orders issued during the first month of presidency	Number of executive orders issued during the first 100 days of presidency
Biden	32	42
Trump	12	33
Obama	16	19
G. W. Bush	7	11
Clinton	6	13
G. H. W. Bush	2	11
Reagan	5	18
Carter	7	16
Ford	5	15
Nixon	5	26
Johnson	7	23
Kennedy	7	20
Eisenhower	6	25
Roosevelt	35	99

Source: NPR

Table 3.2 What policy areas did Biden act on during his first 100 days in office?

Policy area	Total number of executive actions	Number of executive actions that reversed a previous action
Coronavirus	13	2
Immigration	2	10
Equity	8	2
Economy	4	3
Environment	3	2
National security	5	0
Other	2	1
Healthcare	1	1
Labour	1	1
Census	0	1
Ethics	1	0
Regulation	0	1

Source: CNN

Table 3.3 Notable executive actions in Biden's first 100 days

Date	Executive action	Policy area	Detail	Reversal?
20/01/21	Proclamation	Immigration	Stopped the construction of the border wall by ending the national emergency that Trump called to fund it.	Yes
20/01/21	Proclamation	Immigration	Reversed the ('travel ban') restrictions on entry to the USA for passport holders from seven predominantly Muslim countries.	Yes
20/01/21	Presidential memorandum	Immigration	Preserved the Deferred Action for Childhood Arrivals (DACA) programme from the Obama presidency, which shields undocumented child migrants from deportation. Trump had halted the programme.	No
20/01/21	Executive order	Equity	Prevented workplace discrimination on the grounds of gender identity or sexual preference.	No
20/01/21	Executive order	Environment	Cancelled the Keystone XL pipeline and made over 100 other environmental policy reversals.	Yes

Date	Executive action	Policy area	Detail	Reversal?
20/01/21	Other	Environment	Rejoined the Paris Climate Accord.	Yes
25/01/21	Executive order	Equity	Reversed the ban on transgender individuals joining the US military.	Yes
08/03/21	Executive order	Equity	Reaffirmed students' rights to an education free from discrimination on grounds of sex, sexual orientation or gender identity.	No
27/04/21	Executive order	Labour	Raised federal minimum wage from $10.95 to $15 an hour from 2022.	No

Biden's use of executive action is useful when considering the power of the US president. On his first day in office Biden was able to reverse many of Trump's policies and make several of his own without any input from Congress. This is a good example of the stretching of implied powers. It also reveals the different positions of the parties and presidents on policy areas including the environment, immigration and equity, and LGBTQ+ people rights, all of which Biden prioritised during the first year in office, and especially the first 100 days.

However, the limitations of executive action are clear when considering how easily Biden undid much of Trump's legacy. The use of executive action may appear to enhance presidential power and reduce the need for congressional support; however, actions are often short-lived, only lasting the length of that presidency.

Legislative victories in the first 100 days

Table 3.4 compares legislative victories for presidents since 1980 in their first 100 days.

Table 3.4 Presidential legislative victories in the first 100 days

President	New laws signed in first 100 days
Biden	11
Trump	28
Obama	14
G. W. Bush	7
Clinton	22
G. H. W. Bush	18
Reagan	9

Source: NPR

It is important when looking at data to analyse the nature of what was passed during the first 100 days of a presidency, rather than simply how many bills were passed. For example, it may appear that Biden was less successful than his predecessors, but Biden managed to get Congress to pass a significant coronavirus relief bill.

Earlier presidents such as Eisenhower and Roosevelt passed 53 and 76 bills respectively in their first 100 days, but no president has matched this number in recent decades.

American Rescue Plan Act (Covid Relief Bill)

The American Rescue Plan Act was a $1.9 trillion coronavirus relief bill, which was signed into law by Biden on 11 March 2021.

- The bill passed 50–49 in the Senate (along party lines) and 220–211 in the House of Representatives. Not a single Republican representative supported the bill. Every Democrat representative supported it except Jared Golden (ME-2) who had concerns about the cost of the bill.
- The bill was able to pass without Republican support in the Senate after the Senate voted 50–49 to allow the bill to pass using the process of reconciliation, which means that only a simple majority vote is needed for spending bills. This avoids the filibuster — a device by which senators can attempt to talk a bill to death, deriving from their right to unlimited debate.
- Biden had to make concessions to get the bill passed, including reducing the unemployment benefit from $400 per week to $300. Biden personally called Joe Manchin (D-WV) to ensure his support, as Manchin was against the initial $400 figure. Biden also met with nine Republican senators in his Oval Office to try to secure their support.
- Independent senator Bernie Sanders (I-VT) failed to have his amendment passed, which would have increased the federal minimum wage to $15 per hour, after eight Democrat senators and every Republican senator voted against it. However, Biden later passed this as an executive order to appease the left of the Democratic Party.

This case study is useful when considering presidential power, persuasion and relations with Congress and the party. The compromise with representatives from different wings of the Democratic Party, such as Joe Manchin (D-WV), and the need to meet members of the other party to secure the necessary support to pass bills, reveals how important persuasion is as a presidential power. It also shows the need for presidents to keep all wings of their party on side, especially if their party has narrow majorities in the House and the Senate, as in Biden's case.

Juneteenth

- Biden persuaded Congress to pass the Juneteenth National Independence Day Act to make 'Juneteenth' (19 June) a federal holiday. This celebrates the day in 1865 when the final enslaved African-Americans were freed after the American Civil War.

- The bill passed by 415–14 in the House of Representatives and by unanimous consent in the Senate. Biden signed the bill into law on 17 June 2021.
- This was a partial success — it was important symbolically to illustrate Biden's commitment to black rights, but it failed to deal with the pressing issues facing black Americans in 2021, such as immigration, voting reform, police reform and the protection of minority rights.
- This is a useful example when considering the effectiveness of Congress. It may appear that Congress is fulfilling its legislative function by passing a bipartisan piece of legislation and showing the parties working together, but in reality, it fails to address many issues facing the USA.

Legislative difficulties after 100 days

Infrastructure Investment and Jobs Act and Budget Reconciliation Bill

- Biden struggled to pass the necessary bills in Congress to deliver his 'Build Back Better' plan in 2021.
- In August 2021, Biden received support for the Infrastructure Investment and Jobs part of the plan, which contained $1 trillion of funding for infrastructure projects, from 69 senators. This included support from 19 Republican senators, a combination of moderate senators such as Susan Collins (R-ME) and Lisa Murkowski (R-AK) and more conservative senators such as the Senate minority leader Mitch McConnell (R-KY). Ten senators helped to craft the bill, led by Rob Portman (R-OH) and Kyrsten Sinema (D-AZ), to ensure it received bipartisan support. The bill contained many concessions to get the support needed for it to pass. Tom Cotton's (R-AR) Stop CRT amendment to the bill, which banned government money from being used to teach 'critical race theory' in schools, passed by 50–49 in the Senate after Joe Manchin (D-WV) joined every Republican senator to support it.
- However, Biden had much more difficulty getting Congress to agree on the funding for the welfare, social care and climate aspects of his 'Build Back Better' plan. Votes on this were repeatedly delayed due to divisions within the Democratic Party.
- In the House, Speaker Nancy Pelosi ignored pleas from the co-chairs of the bipartisan House Problem Solvers Caucus, Josh Gottheimer (D-NJ-5) and Brian Fitzpatrick (R-PA-1), for a stand-alone vote on the infrastructure bill that had already received support from 19 senators. Pelosi argued that the House of Representatives would not pass one bill relating to the 'Build Back Better' plan without the other; by putting the bills together, it was more likely that the more divisive budget bill would receive the support necessary for it to pass. Alexandria Ocasio-Cortez (D-NY-14) and Pramila Jayapal (D-WA-7), who chairs the progressive left-leaning Congressional Progressive Caucus, agreed with Pelosi.
- However, a stand-alone vote was held on the infrastructure bill on 5 November 2021 after divisions within the Democrat Party threatened to derail the

bill. Speaker Nancy Pelosi backtracked and forced through the vote in the House, to ensure at least the infrastructure aspect of the plan was passed, after conceding to the centrist Democrats who wanted longer to consider the spending aspect of the package.

- The bill, which the Senate had agreed in August 2021, passed in the House 228–206 after receiving support from 13 House Republicans who supported the plans.
- However, six House Democrats voted against the bill. All six, Alexandria Ocasio-Cortez (D-NY-14), Ilhan Omar (D-MN-5), Ayanna Pressley (D-MA-7), Rashida Tlaib (D-MI-13), Jamaal Bowman (D-NY-16) and Cori Bush (D-MO-1), are part of the six-member progressive left-wing 'squad'.
- The left-wing progressive caucus within the Democrat Party was unhappy that a vote on the infrastructure bill was taken without a vote on the budget bill, which included $1.75 trillion of funding for climate change and social care projects. Those on the left-wing of the party argued that passing the two bills separately would result in further cuts to the 'Build Back Better' plan, which had already faced a number of cuts to adult education and national paid parental and medical leave.
- A compromise was made after centrist Democrats promised to vote on the social care and climate change package later in November. This resulted in Pramila Jayapal (D-WA-7) and other members of the Congressional Progressive Caucus agreeing to support a stand-alone vote on the infrastructure bill.
- The passage of the bill was an important legislative victory for Biden who had to personally intervene at the last minute, by calling for unity from his party, to get the bill passed. It was especially important after the Democrats had lost significant support in the Virginia state elections earlier that week, which saw Republican Glenn Youngkin became the state governor, despite the Democrats comfortably winning the state in the presidential election only a year earlier.
- This highlights the pressure that the president is under to secure some legislative victories, especially during their first two years in office. Failure to pass key pieces of legislation is likely to impact the number of seats that the president's party win and lose in the following mid-term elections.
- However, Biden will continue to have a difficult time in the Senate where more conservative Democrat senators Joe Manchin (D-WV) and Kyrsten Sinema (D-AZ) are reluctant to support Biden's high spending legislative agenda and other aspects of the 'Build Back Better' plan.
- The Infrastructure Investment and Jobs Act is an important example of bipartisanship in Congress and can be used when evaluating the extent to which Congress fulfils its functions effectively. Congress is often accused of being the 'broken branch' of US government, failing to pass important pieces of legislation. For example, Congress has refused to agree on budgets in the past, leading to government shutdown, and failed to compromise on important pieces of legislation, such as immigration reform. This case study is therefore

useful when evaluating to what extent the US system of government is still fit for purpose.

- It is also a useful illustration when evaluating congressional and presidential relations and presidential power, including the power of persuasion. For example, Biden made personal calls to key Democrats in the House and Senate who were hesitant about supporting such a high-spending bill. He also made a rare visit to Congress, to meet privately with House Democrats to try to guarantee their support for both bills. It is also useful when analysing divisions within the Democratic Party and the increasing influence of the more left-leaning progressive Democrats in the House.

Other legislative difficulties

Biden also had less success in persuading Congress to pass legislation on other issues such as immigration, voting reform and gun control. Although two gun-control bills were passed by the House in March 2021, neither was taken up by the Senate.

Foreign policy

On his first day in office, Biden stated that approval for drone attacks could only be given after being reviewed by the National Security Council. This is important when evaluating presidential power and foreign policy. Biden implemented this policy to ensure that he was in control of military action. It reveals how presidential power can vary from one president to another, depending on how much control they want over an issue.

Biden departed from Trump-era positions by withdrawing support for Saudi Arabia's war in Yemen, reinstating Palestinian aid, and being willing to end economic sanctions against Iran. Biden is also open to rejoining the 2015 nuclear deal, known as the joint comprehensive plan of action (JCPOA), from which Trump withdrew.

This is useful when considering the commander-in-chief power of the president. The president is easily able to change foreign policy from their predecessor's without input from Congress or their own party. This is helpful when evaluating whether Congress has any real power or oversight over the executive branch in relation to foreign policy. This debate was reignited over Biden's handling of Afghanistan in August 2021.

Afghanistan, August 2021

Biden's approval rating fell to 41% in August 2021, the lowest of his presidency, as a reaction to his handling of the withdrawal of troops from Afghanistan. It was the most defining moment in Biden's presidency so far. This is what happened:

- Biden kept to the agreement that Trump had made during his presidency that US troops would leave Afghanistan after 20 years, but extended Trump's deadline to 31 August 2021. In April 2021 Biden declared, 'It's time to end this forever war.'

- Biden began the withdrawal of troops in July, without alerting the Afghan government or the UK government, which also had troops in Afghanistan. The Taliban (a religious political movement that wants to lead Afghanistan but is regarded by many other countries as a terrorist organisation) swiftly, and unexpectedly, took control of the country.
- In a series of National Security meetings in August 2021, Biden was advised by the secretary of state, Antony Blinken, and the top military chiefs to extend the withdrawal date of troops. International leaders, including UK prime minister Boris Johnson, also tried to persuade Biden to extend the deadline to ensure that the troops could help evacuate US and other citizens. Biden refused to extend the deadline, citing the risk of being drawn into a new conflict with the Taliban and stating that he had been advised that all US citizens could be evacuated from Afghanistan by the deadline. He did, however, send extra troops to help with the evacuation effort at the airport in Kabul. He also sent the head of the Central Intelligence Agency (CIA), William Burns, to meet with Taliban leaders.
- Only 26% of US citizens approved of Biden's handling of the crisis.

What can Afghanistan tell us about presidential power?

- The withdrawal from Afghanistan highlights the impact that events can have not only on presidential power but also on the president's legacy and future election hopes. Biden's mishandling of Afghanistan could result in the Democrats winning fewer seats in the 2022 midterm elections.
- It is useful when considering if Biden is an 'imperial' president when it comes to foreign policy. Biden decided the policy alone, with very little input from Congress, which highlights an issue with the constitutional systems of checks and balances, and brings into question whether the US Constitution remains fit for purpose.
- It reminds us that the US president, in their position as head of state and commander-in-chief, is seen as a leader in international affairs and has a freer hand when making foreign policy decisions than in domestic policy. Despite criticism from Congress, there is very little that the House and Senate can do to limit the president in this regard.
- This also reveals how unimportant members of the US cabinet are. The vice president, secretary of state and defense secretary were present in the cabinet meetings, but failed to have much impact.
- It could be argued that Biden's power was limited by his predecessor President Trump, who had already committed the USA to the withdrawal of troops.

Comparison

It is important to look at similarities and differences when answering exam questions about the power of the US president and UK prime minister, and the effectiveness of the legislature in checking this power.

Differences

- The US president has security of tenure in between elections as presidential elections are a separate event, whereas the UK prime minister can be removed as leader of their party in between elections (Thatcher 1990 and May 2019) or lose an election after a vote of no confidence (Callaghan 1979). Despite Biden's low approval rating in August 2021, he is secure in post until the next presidential election in 2024 or unless he is impeached.
- The UK prime minister is part of the legislature and sits in the House of Commons with the government, unlike the US president and executive, who remain separate from Congress (structural differences in the constitutions). This makes it easier for prime ministers to get their legislative agenda passed compared to US presidents — Biden had to persuade Congress to pass his Covid relief bill and infrastructure bill.
- The US president must have their cabinet confirmed by the Senate, unlike the prime minister whose cabinet does not require such approval.

Similarities

- The US president is commander-in-chief, in contrast to the UK prime minister who exercises this prerogative power on behalf of the monarch.
- Both the US president and UK prime minister can appoint advisers to their executive branch without scrutiny from their party or the legislature.
- The power of the US president and UK prime minister can be checked by the Supreme Court in both countries.

Summary

- Biden undid much of Trump's legacy through executive action, especially in his first few days in office. He also deviated from the Trump era on foreign policy relating to Iran and the Middle East. However, Biden faced criticism for his handling of the withdrawal of troops from Afghanistan in August 2021.
- Biden had more difficulty reversing Trump's legacy when Congress was needed to pass legislation. Trump's legislative victories including the Tax Cuts and Jobs Act 2017 and the First Step Act 2018 are likely to remain.
- Biden's most successful legislative victories were the American Rescue Plan Act and the infrastructure bill. However, Biden struggled to persuade Congress to support his 'Build Back Better' plan — votes were repeatedly delayed on the social care and climate aspects of the plan and significant compromises had to be made. Biden also struggled to get Congress to pass legislation on more divisive issues such as immigration, voting reform and gun control. The 50–50 split in the Senate and the threat of the filibuster mean that getting the necessary support in the Senate is difficult for Biden.
- The 2022 midterm elections will be important as they may change the balance of power in Congress and make passing legislation even more difficult for Biden.

Further reading and research

- Watch Biden's inauguration speech to see what his priorities were in his first year as president: **www.bbc.co.uk/news/world-us-canada-55656824**
- Find out more about what Biden is currently doing by accessing the White House Briefing Room website: **www.whitehouse.gov/briefing-room**
- Read 'Biden acts on gun control after pressure from impatient activists' (**washingtonpost.com**). Why is it so difficult to pass gun control legislation?
- See what action the Biden administration has taken to protect LGBTQ+ people from discrimination, in the article 'Biden recognizes LGBTQ Pride Month' (**nbcnews.com**).
- Find out more about the US war with Afghanistan by reading '20-year US war ending as it began, with Taliban ruling Afghanistan' (**nytimes.com**)

Chapter 4

Biden's cabinet

Context

- The term 'cabinet' is not mentioned in the US Constitution.
- The cabinet, its structure and function are inferred in the US Constitution, which confirms that members of the US cabinet are 'principal officers' of each executive department, rather than policy makers, and that they may provide the president with advice if it is requested. The fact that they must wait for the president to request their opinion and must put it in writing sets a precedent that members of the US cabinet are not there to challenge or question the president, but to offer advice and run the executive departments as instructed.
- There are currently 15 executive departments. The heads of these departments, as per the constitution, make up the cabinet.
- In addition to the heads of the executive departments, the vice president is part of the cabinet together with a number of individuals, determined by the president, who are of 'cabinet level' but not heads of the executive departments (see Table 4.2). Therefore, the number of individuals in the cabinet varies from president to president.
- The 'inner cabinet' refers to the positions of vice president, attorney general, secretary of state, secretary of defense and secretary of homeland security (since 2002).
- Positions within the 'inner cabinet' are the most prominent posts, but the importance of each role is dependent upon the president at the time.
- The need for the Senate to confirm presidential appointees is outlined in the US Constitution. It confirms the two-stage process whereby the president alone nominates a candidate and then the Senate must assess the suitability of that nominee before they are finally confirmed and appointed.
- The cabinet, as well as independent federal agencies, is responsible for the day-to-day enforcement and administration of federal laws. Cabinet meetings can be used as an opportunity for the president to present their agenda and for members to get to know each other.

Exam success

AQA	3.2.1.3	The executive branch of government: president
Edexcel	3.2	US presidency — informal sources of presidential power and their use

When studying US politics, the cabinet can often be overlooked or underplayed because it can appear insignificant in comparison to the UK cabinet. However, the US cabinet is crucial to understanding presidential power and the US Constitution. This is especially true at the current time as 2021 saw Biden's first year of presidency and the introduction of a new cabinet.

For either board, you should focus your attention on how the cabinet affects presidential power and how this can vary according to the president, whom they appoint, how much autonomy they wish to give that member of cabinet (compared to members of the Executive Office of the President, EXOP), and political circumstances and events.

A lack of specific recent examples often results in students writing short, descriptive essays that lack the necessary analytical and evaluative content. The strongest candidates will know examples of specific individuals within the cabinet, how these cabinet members as individuals can affect presidential power, and how this has varied from president to president in recent years. For example, understanding more about certain positions like the secretary of state and the secretary of defense will enhance your knowledge about presidential power in relation to foreign policy. The strongest candidates will know enough detail about the US cabinet and certain incumbents to be able to apply this knowledge synoptically to other questions relating to the presidency and constitution. They will also have examples covering different presidencies, so that they can analyse effectively how the answer to the question has changed over time, depending on the president.

Finally, you need to understand the similarities and differences over time between the US and UK cabinets, as you will need to be able to compare the two cabinets for short-answer questions on Edexcel Paper 3 and extended essay questions in section C of AQA Paper 2.

Examples of how to use the cabinet in an exam

Although the cabinet, as a whole, is relatively unimportant, many individuals within it are not. The secretaries of state and defense can tell us a lot about presidential power in relation to foreign policy. Biden's secretary of state, Antony Blinken, was directed by Biden to hold direct talks with Israeli and Palestinians officials to calm tension, secure a $732 million arms deal with Israel and engage the Palestinian people by restarting the aid fund that was stopped during Trump's presidency. This tells us that Biden's foreign policy priorities in the Middle East are similar to those of his predecessors Trump and Obama.

The ease with which Biden was able to direct Blinken to change tack from the Trump era regarding Palestinian aid and pursue an arms deal, despite opposition from Democrats in Congress, reminds us that the president has a much freer hand when it comes to deciding foreign policy than domestic policy. This may be why presidents are more willing to delegate the delivery of foreign policy to others in the cabinet, such as Blinken as secretary of state, while they focus on securing the necessary support for their domestic priorities. This is important when evaluating presidential power and the difference in presidents' ability to dominate domestic and foreign policy.

The appointments process, whereby every member of cabinet whom the president nominates must be scrutinised in the relevant Senate committee and then confirmed in a full Senate vote, can tell us much about the president's relationship with the Senate and provide useful examples of both partisanship and bipartisanship as well as examples either to support or to refute the idea that the US Constitution still works well.

Biden's vice president, Kamala Harris, was not needed to break a tie for any votes relating to cabinet appointees despite the Senate being evenly balanced 50–50 between the parties. This is unlike Trump's vice president, Mike Pence, who was the first ever vice president needed to break a tied vote for a cabinet nominee after Betsy DeVos failed to secure more than 50 votes to support her nomination as secretary of education due to her lack of experience. This is important as it suggests that the separation of powers remains effective and that the vice president, as a member of the executive branch, is not wielding unnecessary influence in the Senate.

Focusing on the committee stage of scrutinising cabinet nominees can provide useful current examples of effective oversight in action and synopticity. Biden's secretary of defense, Lloyd Austin, was approved unanimously in the Senate Armed Services Committee, and the Armed Services Committees in both the House and the Senate unanimously granted Austin a waiver, allowing him to take the post without having to wait the usual 7 years after active service in the military before taking the job. This conveys a rare moment of bipartisanship in Congress, and senators working together across the aisle, which is a useful contrast to the many examples of increasing hyper-partisanship.

Looking at the social composition of the cabinet can often tell us something about the president's priorities and commitment to representing a variety of groups in the USA (see pages 46–47). Finally, the cabinet needs to be understood in relation to other institutions, especially EXOP, as members of the cabinet can be marginalised or side-lined by the president in favour of advisers, who do not need to be confirmed by the Senate and whose role is to provide the president with advice and help. The strongest candidates are aware that this is less of a problem in the USA than in the UK, as the US cabinet is not a policy-making body. Nevertheless, it is still important when we consider the importance of the US cabinet in relation to presidential power.

How and why Biden's cabinet members were chosen

It might be a surprise, given how partisan Congress has become, that many of Biden's cabinet nominees were confirmed by the Senate with an overwhelming majority (see Table 4.1).

Table 4.1 Heads of the executive agencies, 2021

Cabinet position	Name	Senate confirmation vote
Secretary of State	Antony Blinken	78–22
Secretary of the Treasury	Janet Yellen	84–15
Secretary of Defense	Lloyd Austin	93–2
Attorney General	Merrick Garland	70–30
Secretary of the Interior	Deb Haaland	51–40
Secretary of Agriculture	Tom Vilsack	92–7
Secretary of Commerce	Gina Raimondo	84–15
Secretary of Labor	Marty Walsh	68–29
Secretary of Health and Human Services	Xavier Becerra	50–49

Cabinet position	Name	Senate confirmation vote
Secretary of Housing and Urban Development	Marcia Fudge	66–34
Secretary of Transportation	Pete Buttigieg	86–13
Secretary of Energy	Jennifer Granholm	64–35
Secretary of Education	Miguel Cardona	64–33
Secretary of Veterans Affairs	Denis McDonough	87–7
Secretary of Homeland Security	Alejandro Mayorkas	56–43

Source: Ballotpedia

This is useful when evaluating the importance of the cabinet. The ease with which Biden's nominees were confirmed, and the lack of effort made by the Republicans to block them, could be used to confirm the view that the US cabinet is not very important. In addition, the few examples of Republican senators repeatedly blocking Biden's appointments can be used to evaluate current divisions within the parties. The parties are much less likely to vote as a block in the Senate when it comes to appointments as compared with legislation. Senator Josh Hawley (R-MO) opposed 19 of Biden's cabinet nominees, but many other Republicans supported them. Susan Collins (R-ME) supported Xavier Becerra's nomination as secretary of health and human services, despite his support for abortion rights and lack of experience as a healthcare professional. Without this act of bipartisanship, Becerra would not have been confirmed. This provides us with a recent example of differing views within the Republican Party in the Senate — moderate Republican Collins and more ideological Republican Hawley.

Cabinet nominees withdrawn and rejected

It is extremely rare for cabinet nominees to be withdrawn and it is even rarer for a cabinet nominee to be rejected by the Senate. The last time this happened was in 1989 when President George H. W. Bush nominated John Tower, a former US senator, to be secretary of defense. He was investigated over claims of drunkenness, womanising and ties with defence contractors. The Senate rejected Tower by a vote of 53–47.

There is usually a specific reason why nominations are withdrawn, rather than it simply being due to partisan pressure. Nominees tend to be withdrawn if it becomes clear that they will not receive the necessary votes in the Senate committee or final Senate vote. Lack of support for nominees tends to centre around personal scandals (partly contributing to two resignations in the Trump cabinet in 2017) or lack of experience.

The case of Neera Tanden is a useful example of presidential power and the ability of the president to bypass Congress when needed, highlighting a flaw with the constitutional system of checks and balances. Biden nominated Neera

Tanden as director of the Office of Management and Budget, but she withdrew from the nomination process after facing opposition from both Democrat and Republican senators over messages she had tweeted during her time as an adviser to Hillary Clinton. The messages criticised a number of Republican senators and Democrat presidential candidate and senator Bernie Sanders. Subsequently, Biden appointed Tanden as one of his advisers, as advisers and members of EXOP do not require Senate approval.

Table 4.2 Cabinet-level positions under President Biden

Cabinet-level official position	Name	Senate confirmation vote
Administrator of the Environmental Protection Agency	Michael S. Regan	66–34
Director of the Office of Management and Budget	Shalanda Young (acting)	To be decided
Director of National Intelligence	Avril Haines	84–10
US trade representative	Katherine Tai	98–0
US ambassador to the United Nations	Linda Thomas-Greenfield	78–20
Chair of the Council of Economic Advisors	Cecilia Rouse	95–4
Administrator of the Small Business Administration	Isabel Guzman	81–17
Director of the Office of Science and Technology Policy and Science Advisor to the President	Eric Lander	Voice vote

Factors to consider when choosing a cabinet

There are many factors that a president must consider when choosing their cabinet. Four of the most important are:

- the composition of the Senate, which affects whether their nominees will be confirmed
- the individuals' background and experience, which determine their suitability for the post
- their links to Congress, which help ensure the smooth passage of legislation
- and finally, whether the cabinet 'looks like America'.

The composition of the Senate is an important factor to consider as the president remains vulnerable, even with a majority. President Biden needed the support of all 50 of his Democrat senators, or some Republican senators, to ensure that his cabinet nominees were not rejected. If Biden had a larger majority, he could have been less cautious in his selection. Biden needed to ensure that none of his nominees would be opposed by his own party and had to consider whether he could secure support from some moderate senators among the Republicans. This is useful when evaluating presidential power as it reveals the limitations that a president faces when nominating their cabinet. These limitations are more

problematic for presidents further into their presidency, who may lose support from some of their own senators and/ or control of the Senate. It confirms the importance of having your party on side. This is useful when evaluating factors that affect presidential power, such as the party and what point in the presidency the incumbent has reached.

If the nominee has experience of the post, they are more likely to be confirmed as they will be seen as potentially more competent and predictable. This constrains presidential power as presidents are prevented from nominating individuals simply as a reward.

Links to Congress have become a more important factor in recent years due to the contentious issue of healthcare reform. The president may need the secretary of health and human services to persuade Congress to support or oppose a healthcare bill. Xavier Becerra's 24 years' experience in Congress was a significant factor in Biden nominating him to this post.

Ever since President Clinton vowed to ensure that his administration 'looks like America', presidents have been under pressure to do the same. Biden promised to appoint the most diverse cabinet in US history, saying in a speech in December 2020, 'building a diverse team will lead to better outcomes and more effective solutions to address the urgent crises facing our nation'.

How diverse is Biden's cabinet?

The diversity of President Biden's cabinet can be judged in terms of gender (Table 4.3), age (Table 4.4) and ethnicity (Tables 4.5 and 4.6).

Table 4.3 Gender of cabinet members, 1993–2021

President	Women (%)	Men (%)
Biden	48	52
Trump	21	79
Obama	33	67
G. W. Bush	21	79
Clinton	24	76

Source: *The New York Times*

Table 4.4 Age of cabinet members, 1993–2021

President	Average age of cabinet (years)
Biden	59
Trump	63
Obama	56
G. W. Bush	58
Clinton	53

Source: *The New York Times*

Table 4.5 Ethnicity of cabinet members, 1993–2021

President	People of colour (%)	White (%)
Biden	52	48
Trump	17	83
Obama	42	58
G. W. Bush	25	75
Clinton	32	68

Source: *The New York Times*

Table 4.6 The ethnic composition of Biden's cabinet, 2021

Ethnicity	Total number
White	12
Non-white	13
Latin/Hispanic	4
Black/African-American	6
Asian-American and Pacific Islander	3
Native American/American Indian	1
Middle Eastern/North African	0

Source: *The New York Times*

More than half of Biden's 25-member cabinet is non-white and nearly half is female. The average age of Biden's cabinet is brought down by Pete Buttigieg, who is aged 39. It is perhaps unsurprising that Biden and Trump appointed relatively old cabinets; cabinets tend to reflect the president, and Biden was aged 78 at his inauguration while Trump was 70. The youngest ever president, J. F. Kennedy, also appointed the youngest ever cabinet.

Although Biden's cabinet contains the highest proportion of people of colour leading executive or cabinet-rank departments, Biden faced criticism for not appointing any Asian-American cabinet members to lead an executive department. The only two Asian-Americans in Biden's cabinet are Kamala Harris and Katherine Tai, who do not lead an executive department in their positions of vice president and trade representative.

This highlights the difficulties that presidents have in trying to make their cabinets 'look like America', especially in an increasingly diverse country where numerous interests need to be represented. It is also a useful example of a way in which presidential power is informally constrained. However, as Table 4.7 shows, Biden's cabinet is ground-breaking in several ways.

Table 4.7 Biden's cabinet of 'firsts'

Way in which the cabinet is a first	Cabinet member
First women to hold the position	Janet Yellen, Treasury Secretary Avril Haines, Director of National Intelligence
First openly gay member of cabinet	Pete Buttigieg, Transport Secretary
First Native American in the cabinet	Deb Haaland, Secretary of the Interior
First black secretary of defense	Lloyd Austin
First immigrant to lead the Department of Homeland Security	Alejandro Mayorkas

How experienced is Biden's cabinet?

Biden chose to appoint five individuals who served in the Obama presidency when he was vice president, but he also managed to strike a balance between relevant experience in the field, especially for the inner cabinet positions, and experience in congressional or state legislatures (see Table 4.8).

Table 4.8 Previous experience of Biden's cabinet members

Cabinet position	Name	Obama presidency experience	Relevant experience	Congressional experience	State-level experience
Secretary of State	Antony Blinken	Yes	Yes	No	No
Secretary of the Treasury	Janet Yellen	Yes	Yes	No	No
Secretary of Defense	Lloyd Austin	No	Yes	No	No
Attorney General	Merrick Garland	No	Yes	No	No
Secretary of the Interior	Deb Haaland	No	No	Yes	No
Secretary of Agriculture	Tom Vilsack	Yes	Yes	No	Yes
Secretary of Commerce	Gina Raimondo	No	Yes	No	Yes
Secretary of Labor	Marty Walsh	No	Yes	No	Yes
Secretary of Health and Human Services	Xavier Becerra	No	No	Yes	No

Cabinet position	Name	Obama presidency experience	Relevant experience	Congressional experience	State-level experience
Secretary of Housing and Urban Development	Marcia Fudge	No	No	Yes	Yes
Secretary of Transportation	Pete Buttigieg	No	No	No	Yes
Secretary of Energy	Jennifer Granholm	No	No	No	Yes
Secretary of Education	Miguel Cardona	No	Yes	No	No
Secretary of Veterans Affairs	Denis McDonough	Yes	No	No	No
Secretary of Homeland Security	Alejandro Mayorkas	Yes	Yes	No	No

Experience is important for a number of reasons:

- Experienced nominees are more likely to be easily confirmed by the Senate, as they have the competence needed to do the job. Tom Vilsack was confirmed 92–7 as secretary of agriculture, as he had 8 years' experience previously in the role during Obama's presidency.
- Experience means that the president can allow the individual to run the department with very little interference from them, allowing the president to focus on other priorities. Antony Blinken's previous experience, as national security advisor and as deputy secretary of state during Obama's presidency, gives Biden the opportunity to let Blinken, as secretary of state, concentrate on building foreign relations in the Middle East. Meanwhile, Biden can concentrate on continuing to deal with Covid-19 and other domestic priorities.
- The individual is less likely to make a significant mistake, which could reflect badly on the president. Janet Yellen's vast experience, including being chair of the Federal Reserve while both Obama and Trump were president, gives Biden confidence that, as secretary of the Treasury, she will not make decisions that will damage the economy and affect Biden's approval rating.

Xavier Becerra's background as attorney general did not make him the obvious choice as secretary of health and human services, which is why he faced opposition from so many senators. However, he has more experience in the House than the rest of the cabinet combined, having served as a representative for California in the House of Representatives for 24 years previously.

Only two other members of the cabinet who lead executive departments have any congressional experience. Deb Haaland and Marcia Fudge had to resign their seats in the House of Representatives and trigger special elections in New Mexico and the Ohio in 2021, as they were current serving members of the House. None of the cabinet members who lead executive departments have any experience in the Senate, but President Biden himself had 36 years' experience as a senator before becoming Obama's vice president and the current vice president, Kamala Harris, has 4 years' experience as a senator.

The lack of job security in the cabinet compared to the high incumbency rate in Congress means that very few serving members of Congress are willing to resign from their seat in the legislature to join the executive branch, which is necessary due to the separation of powers. This is because they move from a position where they are voted into office by the people for either a 2- or 6-year term (depending on whether they are serving in the House of Representatives or the Senate), and are highly likely to be re-elected, to a situation where they are nominated by the president and depend upon them for their position — this can realistically only be for a maximum of 8 years, if the president serves two 4-year terms. Hence it is often difficult for a president to persuade a serving member of Congress to leave the legislature to join the executive.

However, it is rare for a president to change their cabinet in their first year. Obama kept the same cabinet for over 2 years, but Trump made two changes within the first 8 months of his presidency, including replacing the secretary for health and human services, Tom Price, after he resigned due to an expenses scandal.

Comparison

It is important to look at similarities and differences between the US and UK cabinets when answering exam questions on the countries' different systems of government.

Differences

- The US president has less flexibility than the UK prime minister when appointing their cabinet, as nominees need to be confirmed by the Senate. However, this is not a significant restraint as rejections are rare. Nevertheless, hyper-partisanship in Congress does require the president to consider Senate composition carefully when deciding whom to appoint to their cabinet.
- The US president also has less flexibility because the separation of powers principle means that if the president wishes to appoint a member of Congress to their cabinet, that individual must resign their congressional seat. This is different from the UK, where an MP can retain their seat as a Member of Parliament while sitting in the cabinet, due to the fusion of powers between the legislative and executive branches. This places the president at a considerable disadvantage, especially as presidents are more reliant on links with Congress to get their legislative agenda through in the current partisan political climate.

- However, the US president does not come under pressure from their cabinet as they are not 'first among equals' like the UK prime minister and therefore cannot be unduly pressurised into changing their mind about a policy decision or even forced to resign from their post.
- The US cabinet meets less frequently than the UK cabinet. As there is no doctrine of collective responsibility in the USA, cabinet members have nothing to say on issues not concerning their department. President Obama averaged 3.5 cabinet meetings per year and G. W. Bush averaged six per year. Unusually, Trump met with his cabinet 18 times during his first 2 years in office. Biden met with his cabinet twice during the first 6 months of his presidency. The UK cabinet meets weekly.

Similarities

- Both the US president and the UK prime minister are constrained when appointing their cabinet. The UK prime minister can only select MPs or peers from the governing party. In addition, the prime minister can face pressure from within their party to appoint individuals representing different wings of the party or to include political heavyweights. This may appear like an important limitation on the prime minister's ability to make appointments. However, like the US president with EXOP, the prime minister can appoint their own advisers to offer advice and expertise. As with appointments to EXOP, which do not require Senate approval and consent, prime ministers' advisers do not require anybody to confirm their appointment and they do not have to be elected politicians.
- Both the US president and the UK prime minister are under pressure to ensure that their cabinets are diverse and represent various groups. Biden promised to deliver the most diverse cabinet in US history but was still criticised for failing to appoint an Asian-American to lead an executive department. Similarly, Boris Johnson appointed the most ethnically diverse cabinet in UK history in 2019, but was criticised for not including more women.
- There is a high level of turnover in both the US and UK cabinets.
- In both the USA and the UK, most cabinet members are the heads of executive departments.

Summary

- The US cabinet provides numerous examples of presidential power, limitations on this power, presidential and congressional relations, especially during the current heightened partisanship, and the constitutional principles of separation of powers and checks and balances.
- The Senate's confirmation of the cabinet conveys rare moments of bipartisanship in Congress — Secretary of Defense Lloyd Austin was confirmed by all Democrat and Republican senators except two.
- Although it is rare for a cabinet nomination to be rejected, an increasing number of individuals are withdrawing from the process because of enhanced oversight (whether partisan or justified) or not being confirmed with the ease of nominations in the past. Neera Tanden withdrew after being nominated by Biden as the director of the Office of Management and Budget due to pressure from Democrat and Republican senators.

- Presidents must consider the composition of the Senate and whether their nominee is likely to be rejected. Although the changes to the filibuster rules in 2013 have made it more difficult for senators to filibuster a nomination successfully, presidents are vulnerable, especially in the current era of hyper-partisanship, if their party does not have control of the Senate — Biden's party currently has control of the Senate, so this should be less problematic.
- Presidents are under increased pressure to ensure their cabinet is diverse and represents a variety of interests and backgrounds — Biden was criticised for not appointing any Asian-American cabinet members to lead an executive department.
- There are a number of similarities as well as differences between the US and UK cabinets.

Further reading and research

- A current list of cabinet members can be found at:
  www.whitehouse.gov/administration/cabinet
- Watch the first part of President Biden's cabinet meeting on 20 July 2021, 6 months into his presidency. Search for 'President Biden cabinet meeting' at:
  www.c-span.org

Chapter 5

The Supreme Court: the impact of appointments on its future

Context

- The appointment process for the US Supreme Court is laid out in the Constitution. It requires nomination by the president and then the 'advice and consent' of the Senate. The Constitution also outlines that justices have life tenure, and can only be removed by death, retirement or impeachment. This means that presidents cannot predict if they will get the chance to appoint even one new justice during their time in office.
- Supreme Court justices can be viewed as somewhat ideological, either conservative or liberal. For many years, the Court was divided roughly 5–4 between liberals and conservatives, fluctuating in terms of who held the majority. It was traditionally expected that presidents would not drastically alter this balance so that the Court could remain relatively neutral and independent.
- The last two decades, however, have seen a shift in the appointments to the Court, and their approval votes by the Senate have become much more political.
- Supreme Court appointments are among the most important thing a president can achieve during their tenure. By choosing a justice, the president has the potential to shape the ideology of the Court for years to come. For example, while there have been 46 US presidents, there have been only 17 Supreme Court chief justices in the same period.
- President Trump was unusually lucky, being able to appoint three justices in just 4 years. Before him, presidents Obama and Bush were only able to appoint two justices each in their 8 years in office. Trump's appointments were especially notable, as he was able to replace Ruth Bader Ginsburg, following her death, with Amy Coney Barrett. This gave the Court a 6–3 conservative majority. Bader Ginsburg was 87 when she died; Barrett was just 48 at her appointment.
- Appointments have also been notable for the changes they have brought to the operation of the Court. The 2020–21 term saw huge controversy over the use of the 'shadow docket', where the Supreme Court makes decisions on emergency orders that have the impact of rulings without actually ever hearing arguments.

Exam success

AQA	3.2.1.4	Supreme Court
	3.2.1.8	Civil rights
Edexcel	4	US Supreme Court and civil rights

When considering Supreme Court appointments, it is important to consider long-term trends rather than just notable individuals. It can be too easy to consider specific examples, such as the replacement of Ruth Bader Ginsburg by Amy Coney Barrett, as important simply because they were controversial. It is far more important to review whether there is actually a notable impact from such appointments and whether they fit into a longer-term trend, or are just a 'flash in the pan' that has notable but only brief importance. This is the crucial AO3 skill of evaluation that is necessary for success in both Edexcel and AQA essays, judging the actual importance of examples that are given against what is *supposed* to happen.

The best students will recognise that appointments to the Supreme Court by the Senate have changed notably since 2005, which reflects an increasingly politicised institution. Some of this politicisation can be seen as the fault of the Court itself, laying out divisive opinions and rulings on matters of national controversy. Some of it, however, can be seen as the fault of the appointment process, with the hyper-partisanship currently prevalent in US politics now becoming more obvious in the judicial appointees.

One of the most common misconceptions in exam papers is that a judicial appointment by a president will guarantee either that the justice will always vote how that president expected, or that they will change the ideology of the Court entirely. There are many examples where a judicial nominee to the Supreme Court ultimately disappointed the president who appointed them:

- President Truman said of some of his nominees to the Court, 'Whenever you put a man on the Supreme Court he ceases to be your friend.'
- President T. Roosevelt said of his appointment to chief justice, Oliver Wendell Holmes, 'I could carve out of a banana a judge with more backbone than that.'
- President Eisenhower said of his appointment to chief justice, Earl Warren, that it was the 'biggest damned-fool mistake I ever made!'

In each case, the presidential disappointment was usually because the justices had not followed the ideology that the president had expected when appointing them. It is important, therefore, not to divide justices sharply by ideologies, or to argue that appointments by a president can be guaranteed to shape future outcomes.

For both AQA and Edexcel you may need to compare the appointment process and the impact of appointments on the neutrality and independence of the Supreme Courts in the USA and UK. For an Edexcel comparative question, it is important to remember that you do not need to evaluate as only AO1 and AO2 (knowledge and analysis) marks are available. For AQA, however, the 25-mark comparative essays test all three skills and therefore you do need to be able to evaluate the impact of justices. For both AQA and Edexcel, the power of individual justices may be a consideration in a range of synoptic essays, including how justifiable this power is in a democracy, the impact they have on politics, and whether decisions are more judicial or political in nature.

The appointment of Amy Coney Barrett

The death of long-standing liberal Justice Ruth Bader Ginsburg in September 2020 created a number of issues in US politics.

Ideology

When Ginsburg died, both the Senate and the presidency were controlled by the Republican Party. This presented an opportunity to replace a liberal justice on the Supreme Court with a more conservative one. Ginsburg had been a reliable liberal member of the Court, particularly renowned for fighting for women's rights. The nomination of Barrett, as a woman, was some effort to maintain women's representation on the Court. However, Barrett had a judicial reputation quite different from Ginsburg's, siding often with the government and authorities over minority rights in her previous judicial rulings. Her far more conservative ideology means that, as shown in Figure 5.1, rulings from the Court in coming years are likely to be more conservative.

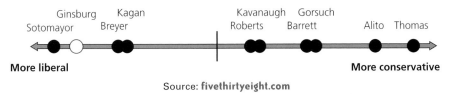

Source: **fivethirtyeight.com**

Figure 5.1 Estimated ideology of Supreme Court justices, October 2020

Barrett, like most nominees, would not be drawn on questions surrounding issues such as abortion at her hearings. However, she is both a Catholic and an 'originalist' (see Box 5.1) and therefore unlikely to be a defender of abortion or the landmark decision of *Roe* v *Wade* from 1973, in which abortion was guaranteed for women for the first time. This was especially controversial in August 2021 when an emergency appeal to the Supreme Court to prevent an anti-abortion law being enacted in Texas was denied by the six conservatives on the Court, including Barrett.

Box 5.1 What is 'originalism'?

The ideology of Supreme Court justices can be categorised in a number of ways. A justice who is originalist in their approach looks to uphold a more literal interpretation of the US Constitution as it was written in 1787. The opposite of this is a 'living constitution' approach, which takes a more interpretative view of the Constitution in the current context.

Her appointment is important for two key reasons. Firstly, her appointment moved the median ideology of the Court firmly back to conservative (see Figure 5.1).

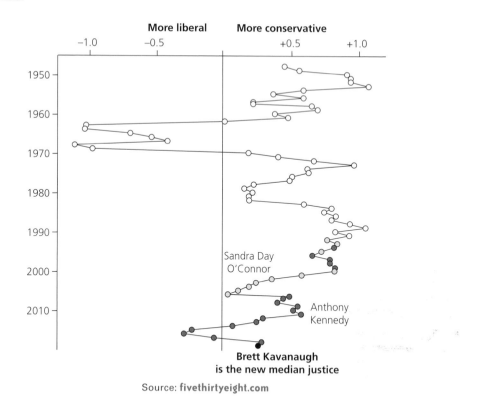

Figure 5.2 The median ideology of the Supreme Court since 1947

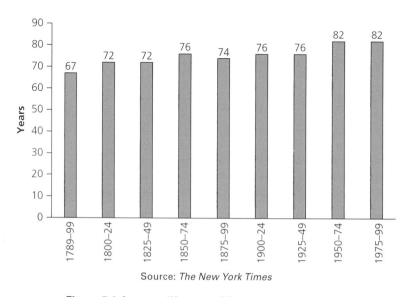

Figure 5.3 Average lifespan of Supreme Court justices

Secondly, Barrett being only 48 years old on her appointment meant that this conservative majority on the Court could have a hugely significant impact in the coming decades. Medical advances have meant that justices live longer today (see Figure 5.3), and it is not unreasonable to assume that Barrett may live beyond 80 years old, potentially serving for more than 30 years on the Court. As Table 5.1 shows, the average time served on the Court by someone appointed at Barrett's age is nearly 20 years. Hence, even though President Trump is out of office, his legacy might be felt for a very long time after his departure.

Table 5.1 Average time served by Supreme Court justices

Age at appointment	Average time served on the Court
Under 45	22 years
45–49	19 years
50–54	19 years
55–59	15 years
60+	12 years

Source: Pew Research

The appointment process

The death of Ruth Bader Ginsburg happened just weeks before the US election in 2020. The average time during the last 50 years to get a justice appointed from nomination was 67 days, notably longer for many of the recent appointments to the Supreme Court (see Figure 5.4). Therefore replacing her before the election would be a challenge in itself. Barrett was formally nominated on 29 September and confirmed on 26 October 2020, with all but one Republican voting for her, and all the Democrats voting against her.

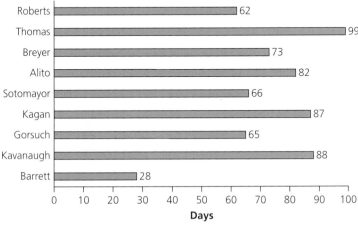

Figure 5.4 Days from nomination to confirmation of Supreme Court justices

This continues a trend of hyper-partisanship in judicial votes that has been more evident since 2005. Before this, judges would often receive nearly unanimous approval from the Senate unless there was a controversy (e.g. Clarence Thomas's sexual harassment scandal). Since 2005, however, the votes have been clearly divided along party lines, reflecting the division in ideology that has become evident in US politics more generally. This is problematic as it demonstrates a continued trend towards the politicisation of the Supreme Court, which undermines its position within US government as the neutral referee in federal and state matters.

The McConnell problem

Following the death of Antonin Scalia in April 2016, then-Senate leader Mitch McConnell had said he would not allow an appointment to the Supreme Court by President Obama. His reasoning was that the Senate had a newer mandate than the president, having been elected in 2014 (or at least a third of them had been). This meant that the public wanted Republicans to be able to control this decision, not Democrats, and therefore the appointment should wait for a new president. McConnell was ultimately betting on the replacement of Obama with a Republican president, which is what transpired.

However, this meant the Court was without a justice for nearly a whole year, leaving the Court with one of the longest vacancies since the Civil War. This had a notable impact as it allowed for 4–4 decisions to be reached, and in the event of a tie, the decision of the lower court (the one that is being appealed against) stands. This happened in the crucial case of *Texas* v *US* in 2016, when the Court was divided 4–4, and therefore the decision of the lower court to block one of Obama's key immigration policies, Deferred Action for Parents of Americans (DAPA), was upheld.

When Ginsberg died, many expected the same precedent to be applied — that her replacement could wait for a new president to be elected. However, Senate leader McConnell again invoked the same logic to achieve a different outcome: the current Republican president nominating someone that the Republican-controlled Senate could agree on would be acceptable, as the current Republican Senate still had a mandate. This demonstrates the immense power of the Senate in trying to control the ideology of the Court, as well as highlighting the problems that separation of powers and separate mandates can cause.

The impact of Trump and Biden

Fewer appointments in the future

The nominees of President Trump will clearly have a lasting impact on the Supreme Court. In September 2021, his three nominees are still relatively young and have potentially long judicial careers ahead of them — Barrett is 49, Gorsuch is 54 and Kavanaugh is 56. Trump's ability to replace three of the justices in quick succession also means these seats are unlikely to become vacant in the near future.

The increasing life span also means that there are likely to be fewer seats that become vacant at all (see Figure 5.5) and therefore Trump's appointments will be especially influential. It is also worth noting that so far, although it has only been a relatively short time, they have proved relatively reliable in terms of conservative ideology, unlike the justices previously complained of by US presidents.

Number of Supreme Court vacancies, 1917–2017

Number of estimated Supreme Court vacancies, 2017–2117

Figure 5.5 Estimated Supreme Court appointments

The Court packing plan

Following Barrett's rushed appointments, there were calls for Biden to 'pack the Court'. The Supreme Court currently has nine justices on it. However, it is not a constitutional requirement to have nine, and it has been smaller and bigger. By expanding the court, Biden would be able to appoint more liberal members. This plan had been raised by Roosevelt after the Wall Street Crash (see Box 5.2).

Box 5.2 Roosevelt and the Court packing plan

In the 1930s, following the Great Depression, President Roosevelt had enacted sweeping changes to try and drive forward the USA's recovery. However, he often found his changes struck down by the Supreme Court. In 1937, he announced his plan to 'pack the Court'. He would appoint an assistant justice for any justice over 70 who did not retire, but the assistant would have full voting rights. While the plan was ultimately struck down, it clearly worried enough justices that they switched to voting in a more liberal manner, not striking down Roosevelt's proposals.

In April 2021, through an executive order, Biden set up a 'Presidential Commission on the Supreme Court' to look at a range of reform measures: the Court's role in the constitutional system; the length of service and turnover of justices; the Court's membership and size; and its case selection, rules and practices. While some, but by no means all, liberal politicians were in favour of this, conservatives were more broadly not. They argued that expanding the Court simply to change its ideological leaning represented politicisation of the Court that threatened its role in the Constitution. Many liberals would argue that the appointment of Barrett had done the same thing.

The 36-person bipartisan committee of legal scholars is due to report back to President Biden in November 2021 with its findings. The review of the power of the Court is especially interesting from a constitutional standpoint. On the one hand, there have been arguments that in making the huge political decisions that it does, the Supreme Court has far exceeded the power that it was intended to have.

On the other hand, the fact that the executive branch of government is leading this review could challenge the independence and neutrality of the Supreme Court, and there are even questions over whether reforms could be made without constitutional amendments. It is especially notable that President Biden has set up this commission, having called Roosevelt's plan a 'bonehead idea' in 1983 and commenting that he would not pack the Court during his election campaign. It is therefore evident that the appointments made by Trump have not only changed the future ideology of the Court, but could have a huge impact on the power and role of the Court, depending on the outcome of this commission.

The shadow docket

Another development that seems to have coincided with the appointments of Trump is the more broad use of the 'shadow docket' (see Box 5.3). This caused huge controversy in the summer of 2021, first because these decisions are made swiftly and with no hearings, but have the impact of a normal court ruling (Box 5.3), and secondly, because they showed the power of the new conservative majority more than many of the cases during the 2020–21 term (see Box 5.4).

Box 5.3   **What is the 'shadow docket'?**

This is a phrase coined in 2015. It describes the Supreme Court's ability to grant an emergency stop, or not, on a law being carried out. A request for emergency intervention is usually placed with the Court because the issue is time sensitive: for example, an application to prevent a death sentence being carried out. The Court does not hear arguments about these applications, nor does it address the constitutionality of an issue. Instead, the Court simply judges whether serious harm will result if it does not intervene, in which case it will issue an injunction. The issue will need revisiting more formally later.

The use of shadow dockets has not only raised concerns about the legitimacy of Court decisions among scholars and journalists. Concerned Court members have also expressed their dislike of the practice, with Justice Kagan commenting: 'In all these ways, the majority's decision is emblematic of too much of this Court's shadow docket decision making — which every day becomes more unreasoned, inconsistent, and impossible to defend.'

Box 5.4   **A selection of shadow docket cases, summer 2021**

- Remain in Mexico — the Supreme Court rejected the Biden administration's request for the Court to prevent the reinstatement of the Trump-era policy where asylum-seekers had to remain in Mexico while they awaited hearings.
- Eviction moratorium — the Supreme Court blocked the administration's moratorium (suspension) on evictions during the Covid-19 pandemic.
- Abortion in Texas – the Supreme Court rejected the administration's application to prevent a Texas law being enacted that banned abortions after 6 weeks and encouraged citizens to report on and sue anyone breaking this law (see Chapter 1).

In fact, this new trend has become so concerning that the Senate Judiciary Committee announced in September 2021 that it was going to hold an investigation into the Court's use of this power. This is especially notable as often there are few examples of checks upon the Supreme Court. As Court justices have the final say on the meaning of the Constitution, it can be difficult to rein in their power. Nonetheless in 2021, both the president (through his commission) and the Senate have launched initiatives that seek to investigate, and ultimately potentially to curb, the power of the Supreme Court.

Calls for the retirement of Justice Breyer

The final impact of President Trump, following the appointment of Barrett, concerns calls for the retirement of Justice Stephen Breyer. At 83, he is currently the oldest member of the Supreme Court. Prior to 2016, there had been calls for the retirement of Ruth Bader Ginsburg from liberals who feared that if a Republican president came in, she might not outlive them. This obviously did become the situation when she died in 2020. There are liberals who now fear the same for Stephen Breyer – that if he does not resign before the 2022 midterms, while Biden and the Democrats (at least notionally) hold the Senate, his replacement could also end up being a conservative. The pressure was increased when Senate minority leader McConnell said that if there were a Court vacancy in 2024, or even possibly 2023, he would not let Biden have a confirmation hearing if the Republicans had become the majority. It was increased further by the prospect of Biden's replacement for Breyer being an African-American woman, which would further diversify the make-up of the Court.

Breyer refused to be drawn on his plans for retirement and hired a full complement of four law clerks for the 2021–22 term, which usually indicates that a justice is not going to retire. However, it is clear that the calls for Breyer's retirement are concerned less with Breyer himself than with the politics of the Supreme Court and the hyper-partisan nature of US politics in the twenty-first century. This again serves to undermine the independence and neutrality of the Court, supposedly guaranteed by the Constitution.

Comparison

- The UK and US Supreme Courts both operate on principles of independence (from other branches of government) and neutrality (in their rulings). This allows them to directly challenge these branches of government and expect their rulings to be upheld, as the UK Supreme Court did over prorogation and the US Supreme Court has over the Biden administration's applications to the shadow docket.
- Both Courts are now also facing challenges and plans for reform to their power because of this. The UK Judicial Review and Courts Bill aimed to make sweeping reforms of judicial review, while the Presidential Commission and Senate Judiciary Committee review of the shadow docket also seek to review the power of this branch.

- The US Supreme Court is notable for its far greater diversity than the UK Court. Having more women and minority ethnic judges than the UK Supreme Court, it can claim to be more representative. However, both Courts are comprised of justices whose educational background tends to be Harvard/Yale in the USA and Oxford/Cambridge in the UK, which is far less diverse.

Summary

- The long-term trend in US politics generally is towards hyper-partisanship. Congress members who 'cross the aisle' and work between parties have become fewer. Political ideologies on the left and right have moved apart from one another. This is also reflected in attitudes towards the Supreme Court.
- Trump's appointees have changed the ideological nature of the US Supreme Court for the foreseeable future.
- Politicisation of the Court has led to longer-term questions about the power and role that the Supreme Court should have, which both Congress and the President are now wrestling with.
- The Court itself does not have a fixed amount of power. Beyond judicial ideologies changing which cases the justices may or may not wish to hear, developments such as the shadow docket have changed their role.
- Trump's appointments to the Court and the way these were dealt with by the Senate have undermined the independent and neutral nature of the Court in a way that is likely to continue to cause concerns in the coming years. This can be seen clearly in Biden's presidential commission considering reform and expansion of the Court, which could have wide-ranging and long-lasting impacts.

Further reading and research

- Listen to the podcast 'How a 6–3 conservative majority shaped the Supreme Court this term' (**fivethirtyeight.com**) and use this to help you judge the significance of ideology on the Supreme Court.
- Read 'The Supreme Court might have three swing justices now' (**fivethirtyeight.com**). Look at the Martin-Quinn judicial ideology scores. What does it suggest about the Supreme Court that justices can be ranked in this way?
- Read 'A Supreme Court term marked by a conservative majority in flux' (**nytimes.com**) and review the changes in judicial ideology on the Supreme Court since the addition of Justice Barrett.
- Read 'From "bonehead idea" to studying it: Joe Biden's shifting positions on court packing' (**forbes.com**) and compare the challenges that President Biden faces to those faced by President Roosevelt.
- Read 'The Supreme Court justices' political leanings: a guide to the 2021 Court' (**mic.com**) for a small case study on each justice currently on the Court.

Chapter 6

The Supreme Court 2020–21: an exercise in fluidity

Context

- The role of the Supreme Court is not well defined in the US Constitution. Article III is very short and vague. Instead, the cases of *Marbury* v *Madison* (1803) and *Fletcher* v *Peck* (1810) effectively give the Supreme Court the power of judicial review, allowing it the final say on issues of constitutionality.
- As national events have taken place, for example 9/11, the Court has been asked to rule on actions that have followed. For many years, the Court has been reasonably balanced between justices labelled as 'liberals' and 'conservatives' when making such decisions. However, the death of Ruth Bader Ginsburg in September 2020, and her replacement with Amy Coney Barrett just a month later, resulted in a Court with six justices labelled as 'conservative' and just three 'liberals'.
- The 2020–21 term represented some unusual national circumstances. Covid-19 not only raised some interesting legal questions for the Court, but also challenged the way it conducted its work. In May 2020, for the first time in the Court's history, oral arguments were held virtually and were broadcast live. This meant the public could listen in directly to history being made. It also seemed to change the dynamic of the justices themselves. On one day in May 2020, Justice Thomas asked 17 questions — nearly six times as many as he had in the entirety of the preceding 14 years! His last question in oral arguments was over a year earlier in March 2019.
- The Court was also faced with questions about the response to Covid-19 at national and state levels. It faced appeals regarding vaccines from students in Indiana and a number of appeals regarding a ban on evictions that the government put in place during the pandemic.

Exam success

AQA	3.2.1.4	Supreme Court
	3.2.1.8	Civil rights
Edexcel	4	US Supreme Court and civil rights

The power of the Supreme Court can be seen as largely free of formal checks in the US constitutional system. The Court has the power to interpret the 7,000 words of the Constitution directly, updating its meaning for a modern era. The only formal mechanism for overturning its rulings is to amend the Constitution — this is so difficult as to be an effectively defunct check. The best students will recognise, however, that the Court does not operate in a vacuum, and that even when it makes landmark rulings as it did in 2020–21, it faces criticism, has to consider public opinion and has no way to enforce its own rulings.

It is also important to understand that, as well as recognising the Court's precarious position, the justices often see themselves as guardians of the law and rule accordingly. This can be seen in the number of cases annually which are not divided along ideological lines, suggesting that justices consider other factors when reaching a judgement.

A common misconception is that the Court can hear a case on anything it wants to. However, the Court has no power of initiation, meaning that the justices cannot bring a case to themselves. Instead, cases must be brought by other parties who appeal to be heard by the Supreme Court. There are approximately 8,000 appeals to the Supreme Court each year to be heard as a case. These are called petitions for a *writ of certiorari*. The Court usually only grants about 60 of these writs, meaning that it hears only about 60 cases a year. Therefore, while the Court can choose from quite a large pool of cases, it has limited time to hear cases each year. This serves as at least some limit on the Court's power.

The role of the Supreme Court is crucial to a range of essays for both Edexcel and AQA. Comparatively, you could be asked in a 12-mark essay for Edexcel about the comparative natures of the US and US Supreme Courts, including what powers they have and the role of their judges. For AQA 25-mark essays, you could be asked to evaluate the relative power of each of the Supreme Courts. For both AQA and Edexcel, the longer essays are synoptic and therefore you may not get a question explicitly on the Supreme Court, and yet the changing power and influence of the Court may be relevant to essays on the role of the Constitution, checks and balances, and the protection of civil rights.

Overview of 2020–21: things are not always as they appear...

The addition of Justice Barrett to the Supreme Court (see Table 6.1) led to a number of commentators discussing the likely impact she would have in the 2020–21 term. Much speculation was made that the newly formed conservative majority could overturn important rights such as the right to an abortion (from *Roe* v *Wade*, 1973). However, while the conservative majority was sometimes evident, *The New York Times* characterised the 2020–21 Court as 'fluid and unpredictable'. Issuing just 55 decisions, it continued the trend from 2019 of seeing fewer cases and there were fewer landmark decisions than in the previous term.

Table 6.1 The current Supreme Court

Name	Appointed by	Appointed on	Senate vote	Ideology
Chief Justice John Roberts	G. W. Bush	September 2005	78–22	Conservative
Clarence Thomas	G. H. W. Bush	October 1991	52–48	Conservative
Stephen Breyer	Clinton	July 1994	87–9	Liberal
Samuel Alito	G. W. Bush	January 2006	58–42	Conservative
Sonia Sotomayor	Obama	August 2009	68–31	Liberal

Name	Appointed by	Appointed on	Senate vote	Ideology
Elena Kagan	Obama	August 2010	63–37	Liberal
Neil Gorsuch	Trump	April 2017	54–45	Conservative
Brett Kavanaugh	Trump	October 2018	52–48	Conservative
Amy Coney Barrett	Trump	October 2020	52–48	Conservative

Figure 6.1 highlights the 'fluidity' in Court decisions. Rather than there being a huge jump in 6–3 cases, the overwhelming number of cases were decided unanimously. Even in the seven cases that were decided with a 5–4 majority, four could be argued to have been conservative decisions and three liberal – hardly an overwhelming shift to an aggressively conservative Court.

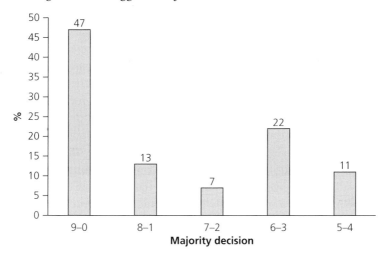

Figure 6.1 Frequency of decisions by majority in 2020–21

Each term, figures are published looking at how often the justices agreed with one another in cases. In many ways, the 2020–21 term not only continued a previous trend, but also actually bucked expectations. Rather than polarisation increasing on the Court, both the lowest and highest agreement rates between justices were notably higher than in the previous term (see Table 6.2). This meant that the justices were increasingly in agreement when reaching decisions on a case. For example, Sotomayor and Alito agreed 53% of the time this year, up from 46% last year. Therefore, increased division and conservative dominance seem not to have materialised in the way some predicted.

Table 6.2 Agreement rates in 2020–21 decisions

Highest agreement rates (%)		Lowest agreement rates (%)	
Roberts and Kavanaugh	94	Sotomayor and Alito	53
Breyer and Kagan	93	Sotomayor and Thomas	55
Breyer and Sotomayor	93	Kagan and Alito	58

The Kavanaugh Court?

Courts are named after their chief justice. This role is not as powerful as it sounds, as the chief justice does not have any greater vote than the other justices. In fact, the only additional power their role really gives them is the power to allocate who writes the decision for the side on which the chief justice votes. The current court is led by Chief Justice John Roberts and is therefore known at the Roberts Court. However, for much of his tenure, Roberts had faced questions over whether the Court should really be called the 'Kennedy Court' after Justice Kennedy, who frequently seemed to be the deciding vote in 5–4 cases and therefore seemed to hold the balance of power. Kennedy retired in 2018, but in the most recent term another justice seems to have come to the fore.

In 2020–21, while still relatively new to the Court, Kavanaugh was the justice who was most often in the majority, both in all decisions made by the Court and in the 5–4 decisions. Roberts, however, was a close second on both of these measures. Of the 5–4 decisions that were 'won' by the liberals, it was Roberts and Kavanaugh who sided with the liberals to create the majority. Both equally had high agreement rates with all the justices on the Court (Table 6.3), albeit more so with conservatives than with liberals. This again reflects the 'fluidity' of the Court in this term and perhaps reflects the position of these two as now being at the centre of the Court rather than as reliably conservative. Indeed, Professor Blackman refers to the Court as a 'three–three–three' split, saying, 'I disagree with the notion that we have a six-member conservative majority on many of these divisive issues.' Looking at the key cases of 2020–21 in the next section, certainly a range of division is evident. It is crucial for students to understand that the role of ideology on the Supreme Court is not fixed, and often not predictable.

Table 6.3 Agreement rates of Chief Justice Roberts and Justice Kavanaugh with the other justices in 2020–21 (%)

	Kavanaugh agreement rate (%)	Roberts agreement rate (%)
Roberts	94	–
Thomas	78	75
Breyer	73	73
Alito	86	83
Sotomayor	66	66
Kagan	72	72
Gorsuch	87	81
Kavanaugh	–	94
Barrett	91	84

Note: Kavanaugh was in the majority in 97% of cases, and Roberts in 91% of cases.

Notable decisions in 2020–21

Voting and elections

The run-up to the 2020 election was fraught with issues of voter rights. Not only were President Trump and his team leading a narrative about election fraud, but also states were trying to work out how to make voting possible in a time of global pandemic. It is in this area that the greatest impact of the conservative Court can be seen.

In the case of *Brnovich* v *DNC*, the Court was asked to review whether Arizona laws that prohibited ballot harvesting and out-of-precinct voting were allowed (see Box 6.1). In a 6–3 decision, the Court upheld Arizona's laws allowing the prohibition to continue. This split was notable for being along predictable ideological lines — the more conservative six justices made up the majority, while the three liberals dissented. This is unsurprising as the laws arguably served to make voting more difficult and it would be expected that liberal justices would object to this. The conservative justices argued that the laws acted to protect the integrity of elections and that states should set their own rules for them. This could therefore be considered a conservative ruling from the conservative Roberts Court.

Box 6.1   **What were the Arizona laws prohibiting?**

- Ballot harvesting — allows for the collection of completed ballots by someone other than the voter, and these votes are then delivered to the polling station.
- Out-of-precinct voting — allows votes to be counted even if they are cast at the wrong polling station.

In a similar vein, the Court ruled on a Californian law that required charities to disclose the names of their largest benefactors (*Americans for Prosperity* v *Bonta*). The Court ruled 6–3 along the same ideological lines that requiring the disclosure of donors placed a burden on donors' First Amendment rights. While the decision itself does not directly affect elections, there is concern that the ruling will ultimately allow more 'dark money' to creep into elections (see Box 6.2). Justice Sotomayor commented on this case that all requirements to disclose donations now had a 'bulls-eye' on them, meaning that they were under threat.

Box 6.2   **What is 'dark money'?**

- Dark money refers to financial donations to election campaigns from groups that are not required to name their donors.
- Donors to such groups can make unlimited contributions to them. This makes it unclear who is influencing electoral outcomes in the USA.

Free speech

The importance of the Court's role is no more evident than when it is dealing with an issue that has only recently emerged. In the case of *Mahanoy Area School District* v *B.L.*, the Court was asked to look at the traditional issue of First Amendment rights, but through the lens of Snapchat. A school student, having not been selected for her school's cheerleading squad, had posted derogatory comments including expletives about her school to a private group of friends on Snapchat. In response, the school banned her entirely from cheerleading for the forthcoming year.

By an 8–1 verdict, the Court ruled that schools did not have the right to regulate their students' off-campus freedom of expression in this manner. The only dissenting voice on the Court was Justice Thomas, who commented that schools had traditionally been able to issue such discipline to students, showing how justices with seemingly similar ideologies can reach differing conclusions. This was an especially notable victory, as it was the first time in 50 years that a public school student has been successful in a free speech case. In authoring the opinion, Justice Breyer drew on a 1960s case in which students won the right to wear black armbands to school in protest against the Vietnam War.

Table 6.4 Key cases from the 2020–21 Supreme Court term

Case	Decision	Topic	Majority	Decision ideology
Brnovich v DNC	Upheld Arizona laws outlawing ballot harvesting and out-of-precinct voting.	Voting in elections	6–3	Conservative
Americans for Prosperity v Bonta	Overturned Californian law that charities must disclose the name of major benefactors.	Money and elections	6–3	Conservative
Mahanoy Area School District v B.L.	Ruled a school had infringed the free speech of a student who was suspended from cheerleading for a year after posting derogatory comments about her school on Snapchat.	Free speech	8–1	Liberal
Fulton v City of Philadelphia	Ruled that Philadelphia violated the rights of a Catholic charity when forcing them to allow same-sex couples to foster children through them.	LGBTQ+ rights, religious rights	9–0	Mostly conservative
California v Texas	Ruled that Texas (and others) did not have the right to bring the case and therefore dismissed it.	Healthcare, civil rights	7–2	Liberal

LGBTQ+ rights

One of the most useful cases that students can review are those in which the rights of two protected groups clash. In the case of *Fulton* v *Philadelphia*, LGBTQ+ rights clashed with religious rights. The city of Philadelphia had denied a new contract to a Catholic foster charity as it refused to work with same-sex couples. In a perhaps unexpected 9–0 decision, the Court sided with the Catholic charity on narrow grounds regarding an anti-discrimination law, rather than looking closely at religious rights. However, the concurring opinions showed there was still division on the Court. Alito, Gorsuch and Thomas wrote an attack on the unwillingness of the Court to go further in protecting religious rights specifically. It is important to be aware, therefore, that even seemingly unanimous decisions can hide disagreements within the Court.

Box 6.3 **What are the different types of opinions issued by the Supreme Court**

The Supreme Court does not just issue one ruling at the end of a case. Usually it issues at least two:

- Majority — an opinion of the majority of the Court, usually authored by one justice but signed by all those who agree.
- Dissent — an opinion issued by the minority of the Court, explaining why they disagree with the majority.
- Concurrence — to 'concur' means 'to agree with'. Any justice can write their own 'concurrence', which is a piece explaining why they agree with the majority or dissent from it.

In any given case, a justice may sign either the Majority or the Dissent. They may then write their own 'concurrence' which explains their opinion on the case in more detail and they can also sign 'concurrences' written by other justices. This means that whilst each case can only have one formal verdict, it might have numerous opinions issued. For example in the 2011 case of *NFIB* v *Sebelius*, there were actually six different opinions issued by the Supreme Court, including three different dissents.

Healthcare

This Supreme Court term once again saw a challenge to the Affordable Care Act (Obamacare) 2010. This Act made healthcare insurance mandatory for Americans — with fines for the uninsured — but also introduced more affordable insurance to make this possible. President Trump's Tax Cuts and Jobs Act 2017 had reduced the fine for not having health insurance to zero dollars, effectively meaning that an uninsured person would not face a real fine any more. A challenge was therefore brought to the Court that, with no actual penalty, the entirety of Obamacare was unconstitutional. The ruling in this case was notable as the Court decided the case had no 'standing' — essentially the justices decided that the argument being put forward was incorrect because having a penalty of zero dollars would not cause injury.

While seven justices agreed with this, two dissented. In making its ruling, the Court avoided looking at whether requiring people to have health insurance was constitutional or not. Alito and Gorsuch argued in the dissent that requiring people to have healthcare was unconstitutional, again criticising the majority on the Court. Nonetheless, Obamacare survived a third significant challenge to its constitutionality.

Over and again, therefore, it can be seen that while the Court decisions may seem to display a relatively high degree of agreement, bubbling just under the surface are often quite bitter disagreements of constitutional interpretation between justices.

Judicial restraint and the role of Congress

When judges act with judicial 'restraint', this means they see their role as more restricted and will try to allow the elected branches of governments to make decisions where possible. This was highlighted in one notable case this term. *Alabama Association of Realtors* v *The Department of Health and Human Services* took up a review regarding a ban on evictions passed by the Center for Disease Control. For many landlords, this meant they could not evict tenants who had not paid rent for a fixed period during the pandemic. For many tenants who had seen their livelihoods disappear due to the pandemic, this was a welcome relief.

In a 5–4 decision towards the end of its session, the Court left the ban in place but with a notable comment from Justice Kavanaugh that this was due only to the fact that the moratorium was ending on 31 July anyway, and that he felt that only Congress had the power to pass such a ban beyond this time.

Crucially, the Biden administration did introduce a temporary ban to extend the moratorium beyond 31 July. The Supreme Court was asked to review this and on 27 August it decided 5–4 that the administration did not have the power to enforce such a ban, effectively ending the moratorium. In effect, Kavanaugh kept true to his word and changed from upholding it to ending it, leaving the decision now in the hands of Congress.

The power of not taking cases

It is also important to be aware that the Supreme Court can have power by actually *not* taking on cases. Usually, a case makes its way to the Supreme Court because it has been heard by a lower court and someone is appealing this ruling. If the Supreme Court chooses not to take a case, it effectively allows the ruling of the lower court to stand, meaning the Supreme Court can have influence even when not hearing a case.

In 2015, this is what happened to Gavin Grimm, a transgender student who had been barred from using a male bathroom at school. While the lower court sided with him, the case had been appealed to the Supreme Court. In August 2021, by 7–2, the justices decided not to hear the case, therefore upholding the decision of the lower court. Only Alito and Thomas said they would have heard the case. This is a good example of how the Court's influence is not limited to the cases on which it hears oral arguments.

Judicial neutrality

The key principles of any judiciary are independence and neutrality. These principles should be understood and treated separately in any essay that you write. A judiciary should be independent of other political branches or interference, and neutral in reaching its verdicts. It was notable during this term, therefore, when Justices Thomas and Gorsuch publicly raised concerns over a ruling more than 50 years old. The ruling of *New York Times* v *Sullivan* (1964) guaranteed freedom of speech for newspapers, by protecting them from being sued if they made false claims without 'malice'. Both Justices Thomas and Gorsuch raised their concerns when objecting to the dismissal of a case by the Supreme Court, and this was picked up by the national press. An excerpt from Justice Gorsuch is reproduced in Box 6.4.

Box 6.4 **Abridged extract of the dissent issued by Justice Gorsuch, August 2021**

Since 1964, however, our Nation's media landscape has shifted in ways few could have foreseen...Thanks to revolutions in technology, today virtually anyone in this country can publish virtually anything for immediate consumption virtually anywhere in the world...No doubt, this new media world has many virtues — not least the access it affords those who seek information about and the opportunity to debate public affairs. At the same time, some reports suggest that our new media environment also facilitates the spread of disinformation...Given the momentous changes in the Nation's media landscape since 1964, I cannot help but think the Court would profit from returning its attention, whether in this case or another, to a field so vital to the 'safe deposit' of our liberties.

This raises interesting questions about the neutrality of the Supreme Court. The Court can select whatever cases it wants to hear from those put to it, but it is not supposed to actively seek out cases it wishes to hear. Yet Justices Thomas and Gorsuch seem to be actively inviting someone to bring a challenge to this case for the Court to hear. This is important as before any case has even been heard, such statements seem to make it clear what Justices Gorsuch and Thomas already believe, which could undermine the principle of judicial neutrality. It also suggests that the interpretation of the Supreme Court Justices can change over time or in response to new circumstances, raising the question of what judicial neutrality actually is and whether the Constitution can be interpreted neutrally at all. Such a response can help to keep the Constitution relevant in the modern world, but by any interpretation is always dependent on the views and understanding of those Justices passing down a ruling. All of this makes the principle of judicial neutrality a difficult one to ensure.

Comparison

- One key difference between the US and UK Supreme Courts is the role of ideology on the Court. In the USA, all nine justices sit on any case that the Court hears, and often their rulings can be seen in terms of the ideology — conservative or liberal — of the justices. In the UK, anywhere between five and eleven judges sit on a case and it is far more difficult, although not impossible, to discern individual ideology.
- A key difference between the Supreme Courts could be their political role. The president of the UK Supreme Court, Lord Reed, is clearly unhappy about the Court being used as a political instrument, and has stated that the Court should apply proportionality 'in a manner which respects the boundaries between legality and the political process'. The US Supreme Court is far more inherently political, not only deciding on the constitutionality of actions by political branches, but interpreting the very document on which US democracy is based and even in some cases seemingly inviting cases it would like to hear.

Summary

- Although there were few landmark cases in the 2020–21 term, it was notable in other ways.
- The statistics regarding majorities in cases do not always show the whole story, with tensions between judicial ideologies bubbling under the surface even when justices vote the same way.
- The predictions of an aggressive conservative majority did not materialise. However, it is only the first term for Amy Coney Barrett, and so this may change in the future.
- Levels of agreement between justices have actually increased and the predictability of the way that justices will vote, especially Kavanaugh and Roberts, seems to have decreased.
- While some civil rights have been upheld, there does seem to be a continued assault on the running of elections and ease of voting in the USA, and the Supreme Court became party to this in the 2020–21 term.
- The 2021–22 term already has some big cases lined up on gun control and abortion, which the conservative majority have not had to face this term. The fluidity of the 2020–21 term is yet to be a consistent feature of the Supreme Court.

Further reading and research

- Use the SCOTUS Blog 'Stat Pack 2020' (**scotusblog.com**) and review the different ways in which Supreme Court decisions can be measured.
- Watch the 2021 Annual Supreme Court Review (**constitutioncenter.org**) to gain a greater understanding of the 2020–21 Court term.
- Read 'Supreme Court will hear arguments Nov. 3 over NRA-backed challenge to NY gun law' (**cnbc.com**) and look ahead to the challenges of the 2021–22 Supreme Court term. The Supreme Court hears gun control cases relatively rarely!
- Read 'Mississippi urges US Supreme Court to overturn *Roe* v *Wade* in abortion case' (**theguardian.com**) and look ahead to a challenge to abortion in the coming term.

Chapter 7

How united are parties in the USA?

Context

- Traditionally, US politics is dominated by two main parties — the Republicans and Democrats. Third parties are broadly unsuccessful due to the electoral system in the USA and the broad ideology of these two parties.
- However, it is often debated whether there are actually two main parties in the USA, or 100. That is because although the Democrats and Republicans operate at national level, their local policies differ significantly from state to state. The Republican Party of Texas looks quite different from the Republican Party of California. Therefore it can be argued that there are 50 Republican parties and 50 Democratic parties, one for each state.
- Both the Democratic and Republican parties have struggled in recent years to find a central figure to help unite them nationally after the ending of the Obama presidency (for Democrats) in 2016 and the Trump presidency (for Republicans) in 2020.
- Hyper-partisanship has been an important feature of US politics in recent decades. Hyper-partisanship means that US parties and the public are becoming more ideologically extreme on both the left and the right of the political spectrum, with decreasing amounts of cooperation between the parties.
- Both parties have identifiable factions within them that appear to have differing ideological views to other factions within their party. In the Democratic Party, these are broadly the progressives, the moderates and the conservatives. In the Republican Party, they are broadly the Christian right, the traditional conservatives and the moderates.
- Despite the apparent division, since January 2017 a bipartisan caucus (group) has existed called the Problem Solvers Caucus. It comprises 56 members of the House of Representatives, evenly split between Democrats and Republicans, who claim they aim to 'break the gridlock' in Congress caused by hyper-partisanship.

Exam success

AQA	3.2.1.6	Political parties
Edexcel	5.2	The key ideas and principles of the Democratic and Republican parties

When it comes to party politics, it is crucial that students have up-to-date examples of policies and personnel. A common error is to rely on broad sweeping statements such as 'Republican policy is to have low tax.' Such statements lack support and also do not recognise that there are divisions within parties over what policies they should follow. It is better to look at the last election, especially presidential elections, to get evidence of the most recent party platform, or include recent congressional action to demonstrate party policy in action. Using Trump's Tax and Jobs Act of 2017 is a better example than simply referencing 'low tax'.

The best students will recognise that the short election cycle in the USA mean that elected officials are often more mindful of their constituents' views than that of the national party. This is due to the use of primaries in the USA, which mean that it is not the party that puts a person on the ballot paper in an election, but the constituents. This results in a party at national level which has a wide range of political views, hence the development of party factions and the comparative weakness of party discipline.

It is also important for students to pay close attention to the wording of exam questions on the topic of party politics. You could be asked to explore divisions *within* parties or *between* them. These are very different questions — 'within' parties invites you to look at the party factions and allows you to judge how united a party actually is, whereas 'between' parties is asking you to look at the ideological gap between the Democrats and Republicans. Note that there is some overlap here: for example, the gap between moderate Republicans and conservative Democrats is smaller than the gap between the extremes of each party.

For both AQA (25-mark essay) and Edexcel (12-mark essay), you could be asked to compare parties in the UK and USA, looking for example at similarities and differences in party policy or unity. It is important to recognise that the two main parties in each country do not correlate directly to one another. In fact, the Conservative Party often has more in common with the Democrats in the USA, while the Labour Party is to the left of both of these and the Republicans are to the right of both — although this does depend on the policy area. For the longer essays of both AQA and Edexcel, parties can be drawn into many topic areas as supporting evidence. Parties have a clear impact on the elections, presidency and Congress topics and could be used synoptically to support such essays.

The Republican Party

The issue of Donald Trump

Following the 2020 election, and the defeat of Donald Trump, the Republican Party has seemingly struggled to find a person or policy to unite around. This was made more difficult by the insurrection at Congress in January 2021 and the subsequent impeachment of Trump (see Chapter 8). In the impeachment, the Republicans rallied to the side of the former president. However, since his departure, party members have been far more fractured on whether they want him as their 2024 presidential candidate.

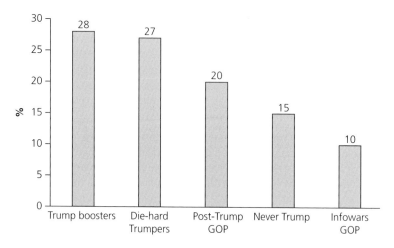

Figure 7.1 Factions in the post-Trump Republican Party

Note: 'Trump boosters' approve of the Trump presidency, but are supportive of the Republican Party more generally rather than another Trump presidency. 'Die-hard Trumpers' would back Trump in a primary but do not believe in QAnon conspiracy theories. 'Post-Trump GOP' would like to see someone other than Trump as the next Republican Party presidential candidate. 'Never Trump' oppose Trump being the Republican Party nominee entirely. 'Infowars GOP' back Trump and mostly believe in the QAnon conspiracy theories.

Source: data from *The New York Times*, March 2021, in a survey of Republican voters

In a survey of Republicans (Figure 7.1), around 35% of respondents did not want Trump as the next Republican presidential candidate, while 47% would broadly support him. Of this 37%, 10% were labelled as 'Infowars GOP', meaning those who not only backed Trump but also believe in QAnon conspiracy theories (see Box 7.1). QAnon followers were among those responsible for the insurrection at Congress on 6 January 2021 and a number of them have subsequently been charged and imprisoned. These figures reflect a deep split within the party, driven by the issue of support for Donald Trump.

Box 7.1   What is QAnon?

QAnon is a group which believes the conspiracy theory that Donald Trump was fighting a Satan-worshipping elite who are currently in government. Beyond this, their claims are often contradictory. They played a role in the insurrection of 6 January 2021, claiming the 2020 election result had been falsified. QAnon is relatively small in terms of its following, but is very vocal, and its members have expressed their support for Trump.

Ideological divisions

The division within the party membership is crucial because the policies that Trump argues for often find support on the right wing of the Republican Party. His policies during his term in office and 2020 campaign were strongly conservative:
- building a wall on the US southern border
- removing the USA from some global organisations/agreements like the Paris Climate Accord

- ending the Affordable Care Act
- pro-life, supporting a near-total ban on abortion.

This means that members of the party who are financially conservative (rather than socially conservative), or those who are moderates, are left without a central figure or policy to rally around. Moreover, those on the very right of the party represent only a small minority of the party membership. For example, in the House of Representatives, the Freedom Caucus is a group of right-wing, conservative members, many of whom have been staunch supporters of Trump. Table 7.1 highlights some of the members of this group, many of whom vocally defended Trump's actions on 6 January 2021.

Table 7.1 Some of the members of the Freedom Caucus in the Republican Party

Congressperson	State	2020 election result (%)
Lauren Boebart	Colorado	51.4
Paul Gosar	Arizona	69.8
Marjorie Greene	Georgia	74.8
Jim Jordan	Ohio	67.9
Scott Perry	Pennsylvania	53.5

However, the Freedom Caucus number only around 40 out of a House of 435 voting members. This small yet vocal minority may therefore not be fully representative of the Republican Party, but while there is still the potential of a Trump second term as president, they remain hugely divisive.

The Republicans — 50 parties or one party?

Beyond the national party, however, Republican Party unity across the 50 US states is also an issue. This was highlighted in the 2020 election in the states that Trump claimed to have won but to have been a victim of electoral fraud in. For example, Trump called Brad Raffensperger, the Georgia secretary of state, telling him, 'I just want to find 11,780 votes.' The call made headlines as it seemed like Trump himself was asking for electoral fraud to be conducted. However, perhaps what is more notable is that Raffensperger is a Republican. In making public his secret recording of the phone call, he therefore made his own party's candidate look weak.

Similarly, the Republican parties of each of the states hold differing stances on some key issues. While there is broad acceptance of key conservative principles, such as lower tax and defence of gun rights, the extent to which each of these is supported in any state varies. Box 7.2 compares the language in the platforms of the Alabama and California Republican parties. While they both hold broadly pro-life stances, the Alabama party's language reveals a much more conservative commitment to preventing abortions completely. In contrast, the California party platform highlights a commitment to prevent only certain forms of abortion.

Box 7.2 Comparison of Alabama and California Republican Party policy and language on abortion

Alabama Republican Party

[We want the Alabama legislature] to do all in their power to protect the sanctity of the life of the unborn, including...the immediate closure of all abortion clinics in Alabama...[and] to pass a joint resolution in the next session declaring that Alabama is a Sanctuary State for Unborn Children.

California Republican Party

We support laws that protect unborn children from partial birth, sex selection, and taxpayer funded abortions, and abortions performed as a form of birth control or on minor girls without their parents' notification and consent.

In an age of hyper-partisanship, when the US population is strongly divided in their political opinion, it is incredibly difficult for the national Republican Party to reflect the values of their members in all 50 states. While the investigation into the events of 6 January 2021 continue in Congress, it seems like the Republican Party will struggle to move past the impact of Donald Trump and find a way to unify its divided factions.

The Democratic Party

A lack of leadership?

It may appear that the Democratic Party has fared better than the Republicans in terms of party unity, being able to unite against the presidency of Donald Trump, if nothing else. However, this is a superficial assessment. While the election of Joe Biden was obviously a positive for the party, there were many questions throughout the 2020 election about whether he was the right candidate and why there were no more prominent Democrat figures who could be viable candidates. Among Biden voters, 57% said that they were happy that he won, but 73% said they were happy that Trump lost — essentially, they voted *against* Trump rather than *for* Biden.

This reflects the fact that the Democrats have a similar issue to the Republican Party — they lack a commonly accepted set of beliefs and an ability to unite around a clear leader. The most prominent Democrat leaders in government are President Biden, speaker of the House of Representatives Nancy Pelosi and Senate leader Charles (Chuck) Schumer. However, each of these figures is in their own way divisive in their party.

- Biden — has been criticised for his handling of Covid-19 and Afghanistan, and by both wings of the party over the expulsion of Haitian immigrants to the USA.
- Pelosi — five moderate Democrats opposed her renomination as speaker in January 2021, and progressives in the party dislike her willingness to compromise.

- Schumer — faced criticism for allowing Republicans to use the filibuster throughout 2021, rather than reforming it.

The $1 trillion infrastructure bill is a great example of the depth of division within the Democratic Party (see Box 7.3).

Box 7.3 The $1 trillion infrastructure bill

This bill is a key policy of the Biden administration. The infrastructure bill looks to modernise the infrastructure (roads, public transport etc.) of the USA. The bill was passed 69–30 in the Senate in August 2021, with all 50 Democrats and 19 Republicans voting for it. The vote in the House was set for late September 2021, but has been hit by multiple delays as Speaker Pelosi has tried to reach a compromise with progressives in her party.

Ideological divisions

The $1 trillion infrastructure bill is one of two bills that were the centrepieces of Biden's campaign promises. The second bill of $3.5 trillion looks to improve social security (healthcare, education etc.). The controversy over these two bills is driven by divisions in the party. For progressives, the social security package is one of their key priorities and they are unwilling to compromise on it. Therefore when the speaker of the House of Representatives, Nancy Pelosi, tried to get the infrastructure bill passed, she came up against opposition from her own party. Conservative and moderate Democrats have not indicated what they will accept in the social security package, but progressive Democrats threatened to vote down the infrastructure bill without promises about the social security bill.

Box 7.4 Comments on the infrastructure bill from Democrats

- 'Let me be clear: bringing the so-called bipartisan infrastructure plan to a vote without the #BuildBackBetter Act at the same time is a betrayal. We will hold the line and vote it down.' (Representative Rashida Tlaib)
- 'We're not there yet, and it is upsetting to me that, as I understand it, they go to the White House and still nothing is happening. So I think it's premature at this point to be passing the infrastructure bill.' (Senator Bernie Sanders)

The comments in Box 7.4 from progressive members of the Democratic Party in both houses came at the same time that Speaker Pelosi was trying to rally Democratic support for the infrastructure bill to ensure its passage through Congress.

As recently as June 2020, some of the progressive members of the party formed a faction called the Justice Democrats. The current Justice Democrat faction has 10 members in the House of Representatives, including notably Alexandria Ocasio-Cortez. That such factions exist as an identifiable entity goes some way to demonstrating the divisions within the party.

The Democrats— 50 parties or one party?

As with the Republicans, it is not just at a national level that the divisions are evident. Again at state level, difference in the language of Democratic parties can be seen. Box 7.5 demonstrates the differences over healthcare policy between the Democratic parties of Texas and Vermont. Each state advocates for quite different healthcare systems, which reflects the culture of their states — Texas being more conservative and Vermont being more liberal.

Box 7.5 **Comparison of Vermont and Texas Democratic Party policy and language on healthcare**

Vermont Democratic Party

To establish health care as a human right by achieving universal, comprehensive, accessible and affordable health care for all and to ensure that all public health policies, including those related to the COVID-19 pandemic, are driven by science.

Texas Democratic Party

Expand Medicaid coverage to improve healthcare access coverage in Texas. Implement an affordable and universal 'single-payer' healthcare system that would provide high-quality, privately delivered, publicly funded healthcare for all residents of Texas within 3 years.

The divisions within the Democrats are therefore notable at both national and state levels, heightened by the involvement of well-known progressive Democrats such as Sanders and Ocasio-Cortez. With Biden's poll ratings falling after events such as the withdrawal from Afghanistan, there seems to be little for the Democrats to unify around.

The divisions between the parties

Ironically, the one thing that does seem to unite each party is their dislike of the other party. In the impeachment vote in January 2021, Republicans were able to rally not necessarily to defend Donald Trump, but to vote *against* the Democrats who brought the impeachment trial. Throughout policy discussions in Congress in 2021, the Republicans and Democrats have found themselves deeply opposed. Indeed, in one survey, 15% of Republican voters and 20% of Democrat voters said the USA would be better off if members of the opposite party 'just died'!

Party platforms

One way to explore how deep the division is between the parties is to look at the 2020 election platform each party advanced. Table 7.2 highlights some of the key differences between the parties.

It is clear that the platforms advanced had distinct and opposing views on many issues within US politics. However, whether these differences are reflected in the actions of members of Congress is a different matter. One way to assess this is to look at congressional voting records. Figure 7.2 shows the Senate voting patterns

Table 7.2 Key differences in the 2020 party platforms

Key Democratic Party promises	Key Republican Party promises
• All women should have access to safe and legal abortion	• Abortions should be illegal to protect the sanctity of life, with very few exceptions
• Strengthening of the Affordable Care Act (Obamacare)	• Repeal the Affordable Care Act
• Comprehensive immigration reform	• Embraced Trump's policy of a southern border wall
• Supported action on climate change	
• Supported universal background checks on gun sales	• Cast doubt on the accuracy of climate change
• Commitment to public transport	• Opposed gun licensing
• Restore in full the Voting Rights Act	• Called to end federal support for public transport
• Require the identification of all donors to political campaigns	• Endorsed states' voter identification laws
• Raise corporation tax	• Repeal or raise contribution limits to political campaigns
	• Lower corporation tax

Source: **nj.com**

in the 91st, 104th and 117th Congresses. The way members vote on each issue is noted and an average score reached for each member showing how liberal or conservative they are. Each line on the graph represents the 100 senators of that Congress, ranking them from the most liberal voting members (–0.8 to 0) to the most conservative voting members (0 to +1).

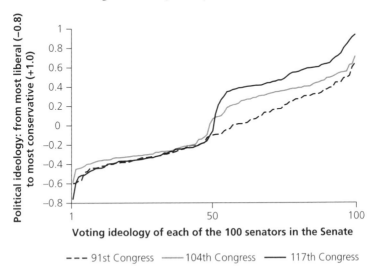

Figure 7.2 Voting patterns in US Senate in the 91st (1969–71), 104th (1995–97) and 117th (2021–23*) Congresses

*data accurate to September 2021

Source: data analysed from **voteview.com**

It is notable on this graph that, over time, the voting pattern has become more partisan — conservatives have become more conservative and liberals more liberal. It is also worth noting that in the 117th Congress (2021–23), the score given to the senators is exactly split by party. This means that all 50 Democrats appeared together in the liberal range and all 50 Republicans together in the conservative range. The lack of cooperation or agreement between the two parties is not only stark but increasing over time.

The recall of the Californian governor

One of the ways in which this hyper-partisanship is evident was over the recall vote of the Californian governor. Gavin Newsom was elected in 2018 to serve a term of 4 years. However, following criticism of his handling of the Covid-19 pandemic in California, he was subjected to a recall vote in 2021 that could have cost him his seat. This was an especially notable event as criticisms were drawn strictly down party lines, and the campaign became one about national issues and issues occurring in other states such as abortion:

- His stance on Covid-19, while the reason for his recall, was also broadly what allowed him to win the vote.
- Newsom spoke out against Texas and Florida both on their Covid-19 record and on issues like abortion, to bolster his own support.
- Prominent pro-Trump supporters spoke out against Newsom, but this actually gained him support.

What is especially striking about the result is that Newsom not only won but also managed to increase his mandate compared to the percentage share of the vote he won in 2018. Some of this was down to him managing to convince Democratic

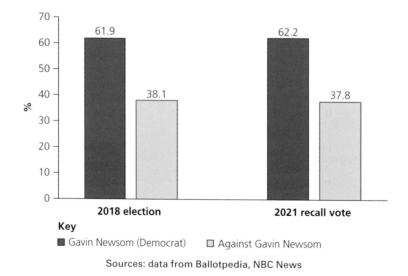

Key
■ Gavin Newsom (Democrat) ☐ Against Gavin Newsom

Sources: data from Ballotpedia, NBC News

Figure 7.3 The Californian governor: 2018 election result and 2021 recall vote

voters of the threat of Trumpism and the need for a strong turnout in the recall election. That the recall happened at all is a testament to the divisions in US politics at the moment, but the campaign issues and the result are a good example of the depth of this division nationally.

Spending chaos in Congress

A final example of the depth of division between the parties in the USA can be seen over a funding crisis in the US Congress. In September 2021, Congress was wrestling with a lack of funding for the US government, which was set to run out on 30 September. In the days leading up to this date the Republicans and Democrats failed to come to an agreement. The consequence of no agreement being reached would be a US government shutdown. The last time this had happened was for 35 days in 2018 when Trump and Congress could not agree funding for his southern border wall.

Much of this debate was rumbling at the same time that Congress was arguing over the $1 trillion infrastructure bill and the $3.5 trillion social security bill. Many Republicans opposed these bills, and therefore used the imminent shutdown as a way to spark debate about the proposed spending of the Democrats. For example, Republicans argued that these bills would push US government spending above the debt limit set by Congress.

On 30 September itself, an agreement was reached between the two parties that would continue to fund the US government at current levels through to 3 December 2021. On this date, however, unless a bigger agreement has been reached, the parties will find themselves in the same circumstances. Even before that, on 18 October 2021, the USA was predicted to hit its debt limit, meaning that it might no longer be able to afford all its obligations and could default on some of its debt, risking a financial crisis. Despite all of this, Box 7.6 suggests the parties are as divided as ever about how to solve this imminent crisis.

| Box 7.6 | **Comments from Democratic and Republican leaders on the debt ceiling and government shutdown, 27 September 2021** |

It's an unhinged position to take. There is no scenario in God's green earth where it should be worth risking millions of jobs, trillions in household wealth, people's Social Security checks, veterans' benefits and another recession just to score short-term, meaningless political points. (Senate majority leader, Chuck Schumer, Democrat)

Democrats want to use this temporary pandemic as a Trojan horse for permanent socialism. Republicans aren't rooting for a shutdown or debt limit breach. (Senate minority leader, Mitch McConnell, Republican)

Comparison

- Both US and UK parties have clear and identifiable factions within them that have caused problems for their leadership. Johnson suspended the whip from 21 of his own MPs who had failed to support him over Brexit, while a member of Labour's shadow cabinet publicly resigned at the party conference in Brighton in September 2021.
- Party discipline, however, is weaker in the USA than the UK. This is largely due to the nature of elections — primaries in the USA mean that members of Congress owe far more to their constituents than to their own parties. In the UK, members are reliant on their party to put them on the ballot.
- Both countries have a two-party system, in which the national party has broad policies designed to appeal to the widest demographic. However, while US political opinion has polarised and become somewhat more aligned to parties, the dealignment in the UK has led to Conservative gains in areas that have long been traditionally Labour.

Summary

- The nature of the two-party system in the USA has always meant a clear rivalry between the Democrats and the Republicans. However, things appear to be becoming not only more fraught, but also more bitter. With public opinion equally sharply divided, this seems unlikely to go away soon.
- Hyper-partisanship in the USA has led to divisions of public opinion, within parties and between parties. The latter, however, is increasingly pronounced with one of the few unifying features of parties being their dislike of the other party.
- Factions within parties are not fixed. New ones, like the Freedom Caucus and Justice Democrats, emerge and have varying degrees of impact for varying lengths of time. These factions are probably more influential when the majority a party holds in either house is small.
- Both parties in the USA are struggling to find a coherent identity around which they can rally their elected members and their party members.
- The impact of Trump remains substantial on both parties, as does the potential impact of his running for a second term in 2024. For as long as this is a possibility, it seems likely that hyper-partisanship will remain.

Further reading and research

- Read 'Party Platform Comparison 2020' (frcaction.org). Note down three issues that could be considered areas of agreement, and three areas of disagreement, between the Republicans and Democrats.
- Read 'How Mitch McConnell has unified Republicans as a red wall against Biden's agenda' (theguardian.com). How important does this suggest the leadership of a party is for unity?
- Read 'Tracking Congress in the age of Trump' (fivethirtyeight.com). Using the data here, how influential was Trump in uniting both the Democrats and the Republicans?
- Read 'How 9/11 changed the Republican Party' (independent.co.uk). Do you think that Trump is the main factor that changed the Republican Party in recent years, or are other factors more significant?

Chapter 8

Insurrection at Congress: 6 January 2021

Context

- When writing the Constitution, the Founding Fathers widely used the principles of separation of powers and checks and balances to ensure that no one branch of government could hold too much power. Having freed themselves from British rule, they were concerned over the possibility of tyranny.
- These constitutional principles should ensure that Congress, the president and the Supreme Court have to work collaboratively to achieve anything.
- On 6 January 2021, after months of unrest surrounding the election result of 2020, a group of pro-Trump rioters breached police lines and broke into the US Congress, causing the evacuation of the House of Representatives and the Senate.
- The events of 6 January were unprecedented. As it was supporters of President Trump who were attacking Congress, this attack was seen as intending to undermine the power of Congress while boosting the power of the presidency.
- In 2021 Donald Trump became the first president in US history to be impeached twice and the first president to be tried for impeachment after leaving office. The Senate acquitted him both times. No president in history has been successfully convicted by the Senate.
- The US Constitution states that a president 'shall be removed from office on impeachment for, and conviction of, treason, bribery, or other high crimes and misdemeanors'. The phrase 'high crimes and misdemeanors' is open to interpretation.
- The president is impeached in the House, where a simple majority vote is needed. The president is then tried by the Senate, where a two-thirds majority vote is needed for a conviction, otherwise the president is acquitted. If the president is convicted by the Senate of treason, bribery or other high crimes and misdemeanos, they are removed from office or banned from holding federal office again.

Exam success

AQA	3.2.1.2	The legislative branch of government: Congress
	3.2.1.3	The executive branch of government: president
Edexcel	2.2	The functions of Congress
	3	US presidency

The events of 6 January 2021 can be used for both specifications for synoptic evaluation of issues such as presidential power and limitations on it, the effectiveness of Congress, particularly in relation to oversight, and the extent to which the USA remains a beacon of democracy after such events. Case studies like this are incredibly helpful for students as it is perfectly acceptable to use the same example more than once in an essay, interpreting it in different ways or showing different pieces of detail from a single example. This lends itself to achieving good AO2 and AO3 marks and helps students to avoid being overly descriptive.

A good case study will enable students to apply one example to many different topics, which is excellent for the synoptic skill. This case study could be applied to:

- the presidency — the powers that presidents have and how they exercise them
- the Constitution — the powers given to each branch of government and how effective they are in reality
- Congress — the powers of the House of Representatives and the Senate, how they exercise them, and the differences between the two houses
- the Supreme Court — its role in the impeachment process
- parties — the role of party ideology, discipline and leadership
- elections — how the electoral process works in the USA for the president
- interest groups — their role and how they impact on US politics.

The best students will recognise that the events of 6 January were unprecedented. This means that, while they were landmark events, it is important to assess the likelihood of anything like this happening again. Good students recognise that sometimes landmark events are actually anomalies and this affects the significance that should be attached to them.

A common misconception surrounds the use of the word 'impeached'. It is important that students recognise that to impeach a president is to subject the president to a trial. Therefore, President Trump was impeached in January 2021; he was then found 'not guilty' by the Senate. To 'impeach a president' is not to remove them from office, but to subject them to a trial over their fitness for office.

When discussing the powers of the president, a common error is for students to apply the phrase 'powers of persuasion' to the ability of the US president to win over the public or the media. Importantly, the powers of persuasion actually refer to the president's ability to persuade Congress, which holds its own sovereign power, to do as the president wishes.

The background

The events of 6 January 2021 — which, like 9/11, have come to be known in the USA just as 'January 6th' — were a consequence of tensions that began long before the election in November 2020. Before election day, President Trump had already been talking to his supporters about electoral fraud (see Box 8.1).

Box 8.1 **Trump on Twitter, July 2020**

New York Mail-In voting is in a disastrous state of condition. Votes from many weeks ago are missing – a total mess. They have no idea what is going on. Rigged Election. I told you so. Same thing would happen, but on massive scale, with USA. Fake News refuses to report!

In addition to tweets like those in Box 8.1, Trump routinely claimed between July and November 2020 that the presidential election was being rigged. In doing so, he set the scene for his election loss and for his supporters to take up the challenge of a 'rigged election'.

Initially the battle over the election outcome was fought in the courts. Trump and his officials launched more than 60 cases about election inconsistencies at state and federal levels, including at the US Supreme Court. He lost every single one of these cases —all the more notable given the conservative majority on the Supreme Court, which included three justices whom he had appointed. In December 2020, Trump lost a Supreme Court case to overturn the election results in Georgia, Michigan, Wisconsin and Pennsylvania, all of which Biden had won. The case was supported by 18 state attorney generals and 106 Republican members of Congress!

Just a week after this defeat, Trump tweeted, 'Big protest in D.C. on January 6th. Be there, will be wild!' That was the date on which Vice President Mike Pence was due to preside over a joint session of Congress which would certify the results of the Electoral College vote. On 5 January, as Trump supporters began to gather in Washington DC, Trump tweeted, 'The Vice President has the power to reject fraudulently chosen electors.' This was something that constitutionally Pence could not do, but Trump applied pressure to him nonetheless.

The events of 6 January

Traditionally, the verification of the Electoral College votes is a predictable and procedural event. Congress gathers to hear the results from each state and votes to affirm them, culminating in the Electoral College winner being confirmed as the next US president. While there are sometimes objections to a particular state's result, these are usually relatively few and are quickly dismissed. In advance of the verification, Vice President Pence issued a statement saying he would uphold his constitutional duty and affirm the election results, despite pressure from Trump.

On the morning of 6 January, Trump held a rally for his supporters at the White House. With tensions rising, Trump, his family members and officials spoke to the gathered crowds, maintaining that the election result was inaccurate. Although Trump did not explicitly call for violence, the inflammatory nature of the speeches roused the crowd, who then began their march on the US Capitol where the verification vote was due to begin at 1 p.m. The events that followed can be seen in Box 8.2.

Box 8.2 **Key events of 6 January 2021**

All times in Eastern Time (ET).

11 a.m.	Trump has a 'Save America Rally'. Trump starts speaking at 11.50 a.m. and speaks for over an hour.
12.15 p.m.	Trump tells the crowd to go to the Capitol, saying 'you'll never take back our country with weakness'.
1 p.m.	Congress gathers to affirm the Electoral College vote.
2.11 p.m.	Rioters get through the police lines and breach the US Congress.
2.24 p.m.	The Electoral College certification vote is paused.
2.24 p.m.	Trump tweets that Pence 'didn't have the courage to do what should have been done'.
2.26 p.m.	CNN reports, 'Tear gas deployed amid pro-Trump protests in Washington.'
2.48 p.m.	CNN reports, 'VP Pence evacuated from the US Capitol.'
3.07 p.m.	CNN reports an 'armed standoff at door of House floor', shortly before protestors breach the Senate floor.
3.53 p.m.	CNN reports, 'Entire DC National Guard has been activated.'
3.54 p.m.	CNN reports, 'Pro-Trump supporter breaches Pelosi's office.'
4.17 p.m.	Trump posts a short video reiterating fraudulent election claims but asking rioters to go home.
5.54 p.m.	Capitol police report that the Capitol building is now secure.
7.14 p.m.	Trump is blocked on Twitter.
8 p.m.	Electoral College vote verification restarts, with Biden's win affirmed just after 3 a.m.

As the violence and rioting took place, Trump was criticised for his lack of action in not deploying troops in support of the Capitol police. In fact, the Governor of Virginia sent state police in to help calm the situation, and both Biden and Pence called for calm before Trump. During the day's events, Trump did not address the nation live once — he tweeted until his account was suspended and released a short, pre-recorded video.

When the verification vote restarted, some Trump allies still raised objection to the verification of the Arizona Electoral College votes (Box 8.3). However, even previously reliable Trump allies expressed their anger at his actions. Senator Lindsey Graham, a staunch Trump ally, said on the floor of the Senate, 'Trump and I, we've had a hell of a journey. I hate it to end this way...All I can say is— count me out. Enough is enough.'

The violent events of 6 January 2021 were unprecedented. The last time the US Capitol had been breached was by the British in 1814. On 6 January, rioters were seen carrying Confederate flags in the halls of Congress, which never happened even during the years of the US Civil War (1861–65). Five people who were connected to events on that day died, at least three of them as a direct consequence of the violence.

Senators who objected to the verification of the Arizona Electoral College vote

- Josh Hawley, Missouri — 'This is the appropriate means, this is the lawful place where those objections and concerns should be raised.'
- Ted Cruz, Texas — 'What does it say to the nearly half the country that believes this election was rigged if we vote not even to consider the claims of illegality and fraud in this election?'
- John Kennedy, Louisiana — 'Our goal to ensure full confidence and transparency in our elections...is a noble one, and I'll keep pursuing it.'
- Tommy Tuberville, Alabama
- Roger Marshall, Kansas
- Cindy Hyde-Smith, Mississippi
- 121 House of Representatives members, all Republicans, supported the objection.

Even interest groups reacted to these extraordinary events. The National Association of Manufacturers, the largest manufacturing association in the USA, called on the Vice President to consider removing President Trump from office for the remainder of his term.

The events of 6 January shook US democracy to its core. In the days that followed, Congress began exploring whether Donald Trump was responsible for the events that occurred, and whether he could be held to account.

Impeachment and the aftermath

Trump's role in the events of 6 January led to calls for him to be removed using the Twenty-Fifth Amendment, or removed via impeachment. Although Trump was not removed using the Twenty-Fifth Amendment, and impeachment was unlikely to be completed before he left office and Biden was inaugurated, a successful impeachment would have resulted in Trump being banned from occupying a federal office in the future.

The Twenty-Fifth Amendment

Immediately after the 6 January insurrection, there were calls for Vice-President Mike Pence and the cabinet to remove President Trump from office under the Twenty-Fifth Amendment. Under this amendment, the vice president and cabinet can provide a written declaration stating that the president is unable to discharge the powers and duties of their office.

Mike Pence, however, chose not to invoke this power despite calls for him to do so by Democrats and Republicans alike, including Phil Scott, the Republican Governor of Vermont. Other Republican members of Congress simply called on Trump to accept the results of the 2020 election and stop inciting groups that had caused the events of 6 January.

The Twenty-Fifth Amendment had never previously been used and would have led to Mike Pence becoming acting President for the final weeks of the presidential term, had he chosen to enact it. However, Pence said in a letter to the speaker of the House, Nancy Pelosi, 'I do not believe that such a course of action is in the best interest of our nation or the Constitution.' As Trump was so near the end of his presidency, it might have been considered unnecessary and might have damaged Pence's standing within the Republican Party if he chose to stand for office in the future.

Trump criticised Pence for confirming the result of the 2020 presidential election, rather than following the precedent set in 1800 when Thomas Jefferson, as the incumbent vice president running for president, ignored inconsistencies in the Georgia ballot and claimed the election victory for himself. Pence, as vice president and therefore president of the Senate, oversaw the counting of Electoral College votes.

This is useful when evaluating the effectiveness of the US Constitution and the power of the vice president. If there are constitutional amendments that are never used, we can question their effectiveness. Likewise, the vice president could theoretically become president under the Twenty-Fifth Amendment, but if this never happens then it cannot be used successfully as an example of the vice president's power.

Impeachment

As Trump was not removed using the Twenty-Fifth Amendment, the Democrats in the House of Representatives pursued impeachment proceedings against Trump (see Box 8.4).

Box 8.4 **What is impeachment?**

The US Constitution states in Article 1, section 2 that the House of Representatives has the power to impeach the president, vice president and civil officers of the United States. Article 1, section 3 states that the Senate has the power to try all impeachments, but two-thirds of the senators present are needed to convict. Impeachment proceedings can be used in cases of 'treason, bribery or other high crimes and misdemeanors', which is a phrase open to interpretation.

On 13 January, Democrat member of the House Jamie Raskin (MD-8) led the single impeachment charge against Trump — incitement of insurrection against the US government and lawless action at the Capitol. The article of impeachment criticised the pressure that Trump placed on Republican officials in Georgia to find the votes needed to secure him victory in the state and victory in the presidential election. It also accused him of inciting his supporters to march on the Capitol during the 6 January riots.

Table 8.1 Impeachment vote

	House	Senate
Votes in favour of impeachment	232	56
Votes against impeachment	197	44

Every one of the 222 House Democrats voted to impeach Trump, while 10 House Republicans voted to impeach him, including Liz Cheney (R-WY) who was the third highest ranking Republican in the House at the time, making it the most bipartisan impeachment of a president in US history. Not a single Republican Representative had voted to impeach Trump in 2019. On 10 February 2021, the Senate voted by 56 to 44 to convict Trump of the impeachment charges, including 7 Republican senators (see Table 8.2). However, this fell short of the two-thirds of senators needed to successfully convict and impeach Trump.

Table 8.2 Republican members of Congress who voted to impeach Trump

Representatives	Senators
Adam Kinzinger (IL-16)	Richard Burr (R-NC), retiring in 2022
Liz Cheney (WY-At-large district)	Bill Cassidy (R-LA), up for re-election in 2026
John Katko (NY-24)	Susan Collins (R-ME), up for re-election in 2026
Fred Upton (MI-6)	Lisa Murkowski (R-AK), up for re-election in 2022
Jaime Herrera Beutler (WA-3)	
Dan Newhouse (WA-4)	Mitt Romney (R-UT), up for re-election in 2024
Peter Meijer (MI-3)	Ben Sasse (R-NE), up for re-election in 2026
Anthony Gonzalez (OH-16)	Pat Toomey (R-PA), retiring in 2022
Tom Rice (SC-7)	
David Valadao (CA-21)	

Trump was vulnerable to impeachment because over two-thirds of the Senate had already voted against him to overturn a veto he had issued earlier in January 2021. On 1 January 2021, Congress overturned Trump's veto of the National Defense Authorization Act (NDAA), a $740 billion defence spending bill. This was the first, and only, veto of Trump's that was overridden by Congress. The Senate voted 81–13 and the House voted 322–87, including 109 House Republicans, to overturn Trump's veto.

The example of Trump having a veto overridden is a useful illustration of limitations on presidential power and the difficulties that lame duck presidents can have (see Box 8.5), despite the assumption that during this time presidents have a freer rein. It is a useful reminder that Congress is more likely to exercise its oversight function during this time as members of Congress owe little loyalty to the out-going president. However, lack of support from your party in Congress on one issue, such as the defence spending bill, does not mean that the party will not support you on other issues, like the impeachment vote.

Box 8.5 **Lame duck presidents**

A lame duck president refers to the president during the period between a presidential election in November and when the next president takes office the following January after their inauguration. Presidential action tends to focus on actions that do not require congressional approval, such as executive action and presidential pardons.

Congressional investigation

In February 2021, Speaker Nancy Pelosi announced plans to create an independent commission, made up of five Democrats and five Republicans, to investigate the 6 January insurrection and attacks on the Capitol.

However, the creation of such an independent commission required legislation. This passed in the House but, despite receiving support from 6 Republican senators, only secured 54 votes in May 2021. While this is enough to pass a bill, not receiving support from 60 senators meant that it was vulnerable to being filibustered (see Box 8.6). To avoid this, in July 2021 Pelosi sought to create a select committee in the House (see Box 8.7), which did not need Republican support, and the House voted 222–190 along party lines to approve it.

Box 8.6 **Filibusters**

A filibuster is a device used in the US Senate by an individual senator or group of senators to prolong debate and to delay or prevent a vote on a bill. Three-fifths of senators are needed to invoke cloture, which is the tool used to bring the debate to an end. However, since reforms to the filibuster in 2013 and 2017, only a simple majority of senators is needed for cloture to end a filibuster seeking to block or delay an appointment to the executive or judiciary. It is still necessary for 60 senators to end a filibuster relating to legislation. Therefore, without the support from 60 senators, a bill could face the threat of the filibuster and be prevented from passing.

Box 8.7 **Select committees and independent commissions**

A select or special committee can be set up in Congress to investigate a particular issue or problem that cannot be addressed in a permanent congressional standing committee. An independent commission, on the other hand, has much broader investigative powers than a select committee and, in this case, it could have investigated what happened both inside and outside the Capitol, and focused on the months and years leading up to the events of 6 January. Independent commissions also have greater powers of subpoena with regard to requesting documentation and witnesses, and can hire specialist staff to assist with the investigation. This goes beyond what members of Congress can do in a select committee. Some Republicans in Congress were reluctant to support an independent commission into 6 January because it would have kept the issue in the public eye for a prolonged period, which could have been electorally damaging for the Republican Party.

Who sits on the select committee?

Speaker of the House of Representatives, Nancy Pelosi, initially appointed eight members of the House to the committee — one Republican, Liz Cheney (R-WY), and seven Democrats, including Bennie Thompson (MS-2), who was appointed as chair due to his experience chairing the Homeland Security Committee.

The Republicans were meant to have five seats on the committee but Pelosi, as speaker, had the power to reject any Republican nominated by Kevin McCarthy, the House minority leader, to be part of the committee. Pelosi vetoed two of McCarthy's nominees, Jim Jordan (OH-4) and Jim Banks (IN-3), because of their involvement in and support for overturning some presidential election results during the counting of the Electoral College votes on 6 January. After this, McCarthy withdrew all five of his nominees and accused Pelosi of playing politics.

Pelosi later invited Republican Adam Kinzinger (IL-16) to be the second Republican to sit on the committee and in September 2021 appointed Liz Cheney, the only other Republican on the committee, to the position of vice chairwoman. Both Cheney and Kinzinger had voted to impeach Trump.

What is the committee looking at?

The committee is investigating the build-up to events on 6 January. This includes members of Congress and the executive branch who supported challenges to the November 2020 presidential election results. The committee is also investigating the security failings in Congress during the attacks on the Capitol.

Committee hearings into the events of 6 January remain ongoing. The first hearings took place in July 2021 and heard evidence from police who fought off the rioters. The committee can use its power of subpoena to request documentational evidence as well as request that individuals attend to give evidence. In August 2021 the committee requested documents including Trump's phone records from 6 January, and those of his close family and political allies, so that it can investigate what Trump told his supporters when they marched on the Capitol. The full report is due in 2022.

Impact of Republican involvement on the committee

Liz Cheney was removed as chair of the House Republican Conference, a group of party members in the House, in May 2021. This was due to her refusal to support Trump's assertions that he did not lose the 2020 presidential election. Cheney had survived a previous vote in February 2021 but lost a voice vote called by Kevin McCarthy in May 2021.

Andy Biggs (AZ-5), chair of the Republican House Freedom Caucus, asked Kevin McCarthy to remove both Cheney and Kinzinger from the Republican Conference after accusing them of spying on members of their party for the Democrats. Republican Conference meetings are an opportunity for Republican members of the House to decide how to challenge Democrat policies in the House. Biggs accused Cheney and Kinzinger of working with the Democrats potentially to remove Republican members of the House.

Why is this important?

This can be used when evaluating the effectiveness of Congress, particularly its oversight function. It serves as a useful reminder that the party with control of Congress has a significant advantage. Pelosi could establish a select committee into the events of 6 January without any Republican support because she is the speaker and the Democrats have a majority, which gives them control of the House and control of the committee chairs. However, the failure of the Democrats to establish a commission, due to lack of Senate support, reaffirms the difficulty that the filibuster in the Senate presents, even if a party has control. It also underlines how difficult it is for a president when their party does not have control of the chambers in Congress or has only a narrow majority in the Senate. Moreover, the treatment of Liz Cheney by her own party highlights how difficult bipartisanship is in Congress in the current era. Members of Congress will be reluctant to 'cross the aisle' and offer support to proposals put forward by the other party if a consequence of doing so is to lose positions within their own party.

Comparison

- In terms of an attack by the executive on the legislature, the closest comparison to the 6 January insurrection is Boris Johnson's prorogation of the UK Parliament in 2019, which the UK Supreme Court found to be illegal. Johnson had prorogued Parliament to avoid scrutiny of his Brexit plan, undermining the power of Parliament.
- However, these events are also quite different. The attack on Congress was a physical assault. Johnson's attack was a procedural one that is commonly used within Parliament, but his use of it was deemed to be unusual. Therefore while both executives have been criticised for abusing their powers, Trump did so in a manner that far exceeded his constitutional powers while Johnson worked within the framework of parliamentary procedure.
- The removal of an executive is possible in both countries — through impeachment in the USA and a vote of no confidence in the UK. It is worth noting that there are two types of 'no confidence' vote in the UK that should not be confused. A party can hold a vote of no confidence in their leader, which if passed removes them as head of the party. Parliament can hold a vote of no confidence in the government, which if passed removes the prime minister and government and results in an election. In the USA, if Trump had been impeached, no election would have been called, but Vice President Pence would have taken over.

Summary

- In 2021 Donald Trump became the first president in US history to be impeached twice. After surviving the 2019 impeachment, he also became the first president to be tried for impeachment after leaving office following the events of 6 January. Trump was acquitted by the Senate in both 2019 and 2021, which means he could stand again for office in future presidential elections. Although Trump's 2021 impeachment was the most bipartisan in US history, there was not enough support from Senate Republicans to secure the two-thirds majority needed to convict him.
- Despite the bipartisan nature of the 2021 impeachment, there was not enough bipartisan support in the Senate to create an independent commission into the events of 6 January. Instead, a select committee was created in the House, which did not require Republican support. Many Republicans in Congress have been highly critical of the committee, which they see as leading a 'political' investigation.
- Congressional investigations into the events of 6 January remain ongoing. The committee is expected to report its findings in 2022.

Further reading and research

- Watch the short video 'The history of presidential impeachments' (**bloomberg.com**). How unique does this suggest that Donald Trump's impeachments were?
- Read 'What is the 25th Amendment and how does it work?' (**edition.cnn.com**). Why might it be difficult to impeach a president today?
- Read 'Fact check: what Pence and Congress can and can't do about the election' (**gpb.org**). What does this suggest about the power and significance of Congress?
- Keep up to date with the consequences of 'January 6th' and ongoing investigation by reading 'Aftermath of the January 6, 2021, breach of the US Capitol' (**ballotpedia.org**).